The Mental Health (Care and Treatment) (Scotland) Act 2003

A Guide for Mental Health Officers and Mental Health Professionals

Bert Calder

BASW website: www.basw.co.uk

Published by
VENTURE PRESS
16 Kent Street
Birmingham
B5 6RD
www.basw.co.uk

British Library Cataloguing-in-Publication Data
A catalogue record for this book is available from the British Library

ISBN-13: 978-1-86178-081-2 (paperback)

Printed by:
Hobbs the Printers Ltd
Brunel Road
Totton
SO40 3WX

Printed in Great Britain

Dedicated to

Sunkanmi

(1968 – 2007)

my friend

Àkàndá Ìràwò tí n tàn Ìmólè sí ohun gbogbo tí ó bá pàdé

(A rare star that brightens everything that comes his way)

Contents

Foreword

Since the inception of the Scottish Parliament in 1999, we have witnessed an unprecedented and much needed explosion of legislation and policy in respect of those people vulnerable because of mental disorder. So rapid has been this process that, outside the policy and guidance produced by the Scottish Executive itself, we now find ourselves with a limited range of text-based reference material. Therefore, Bert Calder's book is welcome indeed, in the context of rapid shift from a Mental Health Act which we can say with hindsight was relatively simple, to the current, wide-ranging and complicated set of legislative tools.

Its worth is that it is intentionally narrow in focus; very much a practitioner's hand-book; a manual for finding one's way through the technical intricacies of the 2003 Act. As such it makes no pretence to discuss practice skills or any wider ethical debate and, therefore, it is uncluttered with anything that would detract from its purpose. Given the complexity of the 2003 Act, such clarity is important. This book simply focuses upon the processes applicable to Mental Health Officers (MHOs) alone, although it is not without relevance to other professionals, who might benefit by having a copy in their back-pocket.

Where, given the complexity of the subject matter, simple clarity of approach is an asset, this book traces a path through the intricacies of the 2003 Act, mostly using the logic of the Act's own structure. In this way it walks the person consulting it through the main tasks attendant upon the MHO. It sets out its text in easy reference bullet-point format and it adopts a formula of introduction to the salient points of the topic, followed by practice points arranged under the headings "consultation", "assessment" and "notification". In this way, even a novice practitioner could pick up the book and use it as orientation to the task of (for example) making a compulsory treatment order (CTO) application.

The book touches upon subjects closely related to the MHO's duties, such as Nurses Holding Power, and it steers clear of areas of complication less directly relevant, such as the intricacies of treatment as set out in Part 16. Thus, in content, the book covers the main areas of the Act for MHOs – Emergency and Short-term Detentions, CTOs, actions under Criminal Procedure and warrants. Within this framework, it makes links to wider points of reference in the Adults with Incapacity legislation, the Codes of Practice and the National Standards for MHO Services amongst others. There is use of handy exemplars for application for CTO and warrants and an extensive set of sample letters in Chapter 9.

In particular, the book has a broad based approach to the MHO tasks, but it also helps to unravel some of the more difficult to penetrate issues such as the differentiation of the types of warrant offered under the 2003 Act. The outline contents for the MHO's report to the Court for a compulsion order usefully separates this report out from the social circumstances report (SCR), which is helpfully outlined in the template letters in Chapter 9. These, in particular, are matters which many experienced MHOs struggle with.

With its new raft of mental health legislation, Scotland arguably stands at the cutting edge. As we move further into the exploration of how to use these tools, we need to think very carefully about training new generations of practitioners. For those of us with longitudinal experience it is easy to gloss over the daunting task of coming new to this mind-boggling world.

Currently I am working with the Scottish Social Services Council (SSSC) on designing a framework for MHO training which will make it fit to meet these challenges and one aspect of this is considering where good quality materials might be found. On opening these pages, it was immediately evident that Bert Calder's book will be an important addition to the trainee MHO's and the new practitioner's libraries.

On the other hand, the MHO role now being so vast, virtually no practitioner can assume working experience of the range of statutory tasks. Therefore, copies of this book ought to sit in every MHO office in Scotland, for perusal whenever a rare warrant is required, or a request lands for provision of a designated MHO for a State Hospital patient from an Authority in which there is scant experience of such matters.

Mike Maas-Lowit (2007)

Preface

◆ Why did you write this book?

As a full-time MHO I am often asked advice about the Act from other MHO colleagues who work in different fields. The need that emerged was for a practice-based guide they could use without re-training. I studied the kinds of questions MHOs asked and built a simple 3-stage model based on this pattern. The model is:

Stage 1: **Consultation**
What is expected of me, for example, consent, application to a Tribunal, reviews, warrants?

Stage 2: **Assessment**
What do I need to know to do the assessment?

Stage 3: **Notification**
Who do I notify after the assessment is complete?

Within each stage are listed information and practice points. The MHO can, therefore, use this book to work through each role (see Introduction for examples of this model).

◆ How have you made up the book?

The nine chapters and three appendices are divided into two categories:

i) **Summary information**
Chapters 1 and 7 and the Appendices. These may be of use to a range of professionals working with the Act given the shared knowledge required.

ii) **Application of MHO role**

Chapters 2, 3, 4, 5, 6, 8 and 9. These are detailed practice guides for MHOs on how to implement the Act. This includes examples for a CTO application, reviews, warrants, social circumstances reports and, finally, in Chapter 9 suggested templates for notifications. The CAN model is used as the structure for discussing the MHO role specifically within the civil compulsory powers in Chapters 2 and 3.

The book references are mainly legislation – the Act, Code of Practice, regulations known as Scottish Statutory Instruments. Also included are the MHO National Standards which local authorities are expected to maintain. Most legal references are in the footnotes at the end of each chapter, for example, section 44 refers to short-term detention certificates. References have page numbers in the Act when quoting subsections. There are also endnotes after each chapter to discuss a point in more detail. They are in capitals as follows: (A), (B) and so on.

Given the unique practice-based purpose of this book, I have avoided detailed discussions on the overall development of the Act or its links with other legislation. Key mental health act literature is referenced where appropriate to support practice issues. I am grateful to those authors for this purpose.

◆ How should I approach reading this book?

This depends on your experience and profession. A student MHO may wish to start with Chapter 1, which outlines the main concepts of the Act. The next step could be to read Chapter 9 that lists summary questions of key parts of the Act. The remaining chapters are more practice-based with details on the MHO role itself.

Qualified MHOs may wish to use each chapter separately as the need arises. There are clear overlaps in information between the chapters and the Appendices as the book is designed for different levels of MHO experience with basic shared knowledge. The application chapters take this information much further.

There is also an optional "what happens next" in Appendix 2, which details legal events after an MHO has consented to a certificate or a

Tribunal have granted a compulsory treatment order. This may be helpful for student MHOs and also mental health professionals.

The Index is in two parts. The first part is a reference index listing the MHO role in specific legal sections from start to finish in the Act. The second part is a general index in alphabetical order. The page numbers only refer to key discussions in the book.

◆ Who is the author?

I have been a main grade social worker in Falkirk now since 1981 initially with Central Regional Council and then Falkirk Council. I started as a Mental Health Officer with the 1984 MH Act in 1987 and have been a full-time MHO now since September 2005.

Personal thanks

I would like to record my thanks to the following team of people whose skills and honest feedback made the task of writing this book much easier: Dr. Susan Anderson, Irene Burt, Stephen French, Julie Hanley, Sue Hatton, Dr. Jane Larner, Dr. Geraldine MacFlynn.

My thanks also extend to the community care team members in Grahamston office, Falkirk Council who allowed me to do a one-year secondment in 2004/05 that led to this book being written.

Finally, to Mike Maas-Lowit, Lecturer Applied Social Studies, Robert Gordon University, Aberdeen for his Foreword.

The law is stated as at December 2007. Any errors or opinions are my own.

Bert Calder

Acknowledgements

The author would like to thank Mrs. Janet Birks, Director of Housing and Social Work Services, Falkirk Council for the use of material printed in Appendix 2. This is a shorter version of the procedures the author compiled for that council while on secondment.

The author would also like to thank the Mental Welfare Commission and the Scottish Executive for permission to use legislation and guidance information in the book.

The author has a general gratitude to other contributors to this field that have been quoted in this book.

Abbreviations

The Act: Mental Health (Care and Treatment) (Scotland) Act 2003

AMP: Approved medical practitioner

CPN: Community psychiatric nurse

CoP: Code of Practice in three volumes for the Mental Health (Care and Treatment) (Scotland) Act 2003 issued by the Scottish Executive

MHO: Mental Health Officer

RMN: Registered mental nurse

RMO: Responsible medical officer.

1995 Act: Criminal Procedure (Scotland) Act 1995

Sections: this normally refers to the Act and will be quoted in brackets

Tribunal Rules: The Mental Health Tribunal for Scotland (Practice and Procedure) (No 2) Rules 2005. Scottish Statutory Instrument reference 2005 No.519

Introduction

Application of the Consultation, Assessment and Notification Model in this book.

1) MHO Role – CAN model of Consultation/Assessment/Notification

The Act outlines the roles of key professionals/agencies such as the RMO, MHO, Hospital Manager and Tribunal. The Act intends these roles to interconnect in most of the procedures. This is not easy to follow given the way the Act is set out and the language used. The CAN model is intended to help the MHO to see how they fit into the whole process. It might be helpful too for the MHO to look at the procedural flowcharts published by the Mental Welfare Commission.[1]

CAN Stages Model applied to consent to civil compulsory powers

STAGE 1: Consultation

Who is asking the MHO? What are they looking for?

A medical practitioner consults the MHO to assess and consent to a certificate/order for detention.

STAGE 2: Assessment

What are the legal criteria for this power? How does this fit with the principles in section 1 of the Act?

MHO assesses the application with respect to the legal criteria for the specific power.

STAGE 3: Notification

What are the forms/letters needed? Who does the MHO send them to?

MHO's administrative duty after the assessment is complete.

2) Examples of this CAN application in detention certificates/reviews of orders/named persons

STAGE 1

Medical practitioner **consults** an MHO to assess and consent to a certificate:

- i) emergency certificate [section 36(3)(d)].
- ii) short-term certificate [section 44(3)(d)].
- iii) reviews of compulsory treatment order:
  - to extend the order [section 87(2)(iii)];
  - to extend and vary the order [section 88(3)].

STAGE 2

MHO **assesses** for detention certificates/orders/reviews/named persons:

- i) emergency certificate: assesses to consent or withhold consent [section 36(3)(d)].
- ii) short-term detention: interviews patient [section 45(1)(a)]; compulsory treatment order: completes a proposed care plan [section 61].
- iii) reviews – offers a view to extend an order [section 85]; extend and vary an order [section 89].
- iv) named persons: assesses suitability [section 255(6)(b.)

STAGE 3

MHO **notifies** the medical practitioner; subject of assessment; named persons (legal references in footnotes):

- i) short-term certificate: MHO notifies medical practitioner of assessment[2]; MHO informs patient of advocacy services.[3] compulsory treatment order – notifies subject of report; named person; Commission.[4]
- ii) reviews: MHO informs RMO about decision to extend order[5]; extend and vary order.[6]
- iii) named persons: identification in certificates/orders. Short-term certificate[7]; CTO[8]; compulsion orders[9]; application to Tribunal about inappropriate named person.[10]

References:

The 2003 Act, Regulations (termed: Scottish Statutory Instruments) – explanatory notes are available online at: www.opsi.gov.uk/legislation/scotland/s-acts.htm

Mental Welfare Commission publication. An Introduction to the 2003 Act[11]

Footnotes:

1 Mental Welfare Commission for Scotland website: www.mwcscot.org.uk
2 section 44(3)(d).
3 section 45(1)(c).
4 section 60(1).
5 section 85(2)(d).
6 section 89(2)(e).
7 section 45(1)(b).
8 section 59.
9 section 138.
10 section 255(6) & (7).
11 An Introduction to the 2003 Act: Mental Welfare Commission, available online at www.mwcscot.org.uk/web/site/GoodPractice/Publications/Mental_Health_Act_Topic_Guides.asp

Chapter 1

The 2003 Act – Main Concepts

1) The Act

Summary

- Scottish Parliament passed the Act in March 2003. It came into effect on 5 October 2005. It is in 23 Parts with 6 Schedules. See 'Structure of the Act' below for details.
- The aim is to make sure people with mental health problems in Scotland receive effective care and treatment in a way which accords with the principles originally proposed in the Millan Report (see below).
- The definition of mental disorder covers three areas – mental illness, personality disorder and learning disability, however caused or manifested.[1]
- A Tribunal system has replaced the sheriff court in deciding on all orders beyond the 28-day short-term detention. The exception is appeals that are heard by the sheriff principal or, in some circumstances, in the Court of Session.
- There are now statutory principles that set out the way functions must be discharged by certain professionals including the MHO, doctors and nurses (see 3) 'Principles in the act' below).
- The Act introduces advance statements and named persons for patients as safeguards for representation should they lose capacity while being detained under the Act. These are in-built safeguards for patients to have a say in how they wish to be treated and also who they want to represent their views if they are too unwell to express themselves.
- Other sections of the Act place further duties on those discharging functions under the Act, for example, a duty to have regard to the Code of Practice on the Act[2]; a duty to lessen any harm to child-parent relations, where relevant.[3]

Structure of the Act[4]

- The Mental Health (Care and Treatment) (Scotland) Act 2003 was introduced in October 2005 to replace the Mental Health (Scotland) Act 1984. Under the 2003 Act the Mental Health Officer (MHO) has been given a more prominent role in coordinating both the administrative and professional assessments, particularly with longer civil compulsory powers.
- In addition, the MHO is expected to express independent views on medical assessments. The Act, too, emphasises the inter-dependence of professions in making decisions about detentions.
- The Act is sub-divided as follows: Parts – Chapters – Sections.
- There are 23 Parts each with a title and varying numbers of chapters. Each chapter is divided into sections (see the full list below).
- Sections can be broken down into sub-sections which are identified by numbers (1), (2) and so on, and then paragraphs identified by letters (a), (b) and then further divided into numbers (i), (ii), for example, section 114(c)(i). Note that the 333 sections are continuous through the whole and not just within each Part. Part 16, for example, contains sections 233 to 249. The book will, therefore, reference sections to ease access.

- The 23 Parts are sub-divided into the following categories:

Organisational roles and duties
(Parts 1-4, 14-15, some of Parts 18, 22-23)

Compulsory treatment and detention
(Parts 5-7, 19-20)

People with mental disorder involved in criminal proceedings
(Parts 8-13)

Individual rights and safeguards
(Parts 16-17, some of Parts 18 and 21)

- At the end of the Act are 6 Schedules that are placed after the main text of the Act which provide further detail on aspects of the Act and some make provision for changes to, or the repeal of, other legislation.
- Finally, the Act cross-refers to parallel legislation. Much of Part 8 and of Schedule 4 that deal with mentally disordered persons in criminal proceedings are in the form of amendments to the Criminal Procedure (Scotland) Act 1995. Some of the sections take the form of insertions to, or replacements for, sections in the 1995 Act for example, sections 130 has 21 insertions referenced as 52(A) to 52(U). The book would reference this as "section 130, subsection 52(S), p. 93". The page numbers are included to avoid reader confusion.

Purpose of the Act

The principles developed by the Millan Committee[5] informed the Scottish Executive's thinking when developing the policy for the Act. Not all the Millan principles could be fully expressed in terms of statutory duties or powers. The Act does, however, contain a range of provisions that give significant and meaningful effect to the recommendations in the Millan report.[6]

The Act is designed to help achieve the objective of effective care and treatment for the benefit of people with mental disorder by:

- ensuring that emergency, short-term and longer-term periods of detention in hospital may only take place where strict criteria have been met and where clearly defined procedures have been followed;
- providing a new forum, the Mental Health Tribunal, to make important decisions in relation to compulsory measures imposed on people under the Act;
- strengthening the rights of the patient and the patient's named person to allow an application for revocation (cancellation) of a compulsory treatment order (CTO);
- giving the Mental Welfare Commission and the patient's responsible medical officer (RMO) the right to refer a CTO to the Tribunal for review where an important element of the order is not being provided;

- treating offenders who enter the mental health system in the same way as civil patients wherever possible, but with some adjustment to reflect legitimate interests of justice and public safety; and
- giving powers to the Tribunal to make major decisions affecting the management of restricted patients, such as discharge for patients on a restriction order and compulsion order, and, for patients subject to hospital directions or transfer for treatment directions, the power to direct the Scottish Ministers to cancel these directions.

2) The main powers of the Act – civil compulsory orders[7]

- The Act allows for people of any age to be placed on different kinds of civil compulsory orders according to their circumstances.

There are three main kinds of compulsory powers:

1. **Emergency detention certificate**
   This allows a person to be detained in any hospital for up to 72 hours. It is mostly used in urgent circumstances and for assessment purposes only.[(A)] Any registered doctor can grant this certificate with consent from an MHO, where practicable.[(B)]

2. **Short-term detention certificate**
   This allows assessment and treatment in a hospital for up to 28 days. An approved medical practitioner (AMP), usually a Consultant Psychiatrist, can only grant this certificate.[(C)] MHO consent must be given before this certificate can be granted.

3. **Compulsory treatment order**
   This allows assessment and treatment for a patient in a hospital or in the community. It can last for up to six months in the first instance. Only a Tribunal can grant this order. The MHO is the sole applicant to the Tribunal. The patient's responsible medical officer (see below), can extend the order for another six months and then annually.

- A shorter form of a CTO is an interim CTO that can legally span 56 days. This is normally used to allow a patient, or more likely a patient's solicitor, time to prepare evidence to oppose a CTO application.[8]
- The patient and the named person may be entitled to free legal aid but this may be subject to financial limits. It therefore depends on the merits of the case. A frivolous application for legal aid would be rejected.

Other powers in the Act include:

a) **Nurses holding power**
If a voluntary patient is in hospital and decides to leave, an appropriately qualified nurse can hold that person in the ward for up to two hours and then for a further hour to allow a doctor to examine the patient and an MHO to give consent to further detention, if appropriate.[9]

b) **Removal to a place of safety**
If someone in a public place appears to have a mental disorder, and appears to be in need of care and treatment, the police can take that person to a place of safety. The health authority determines the location locally. The person can be kept there for up to 24 hours to allow for an assessment and for alternative arrangements to be made.

3) Principles in the Act[10/11]

The Act is based on a set of guiding principles. These help to set the tone of the Act and guide its interpretation. As a general rule, any professional who takes any action under the Act has to take account of the principles listed below:

1. **Section 1(3)(a)** – the patient's present and past wishes and feelings relevant to the discharge of the function. The patient should be fully involved, so far as they are able to be, in all aspects of their assessment, care, treatment and support. Their past and present wishes should be taken into account.

2. **Section 1(3)(b)** – views of patient's named person/carer/guardian/welfare attorney. Those who provide care to service users, either on an informal or a formal basis, should be respected for their role and experience, receive appropriate information and advice, and have their views and needs taken into account.
3. **Section 1(3)(c)** – patient participation. The patient should be actively encouraged to participate in the decision-making processes and procedures under the Act.
4. **Section 1(3)(d)** – provision of information. Patients should be provided with all the information and support necessary to enable them to participate fully. Information should be presented in an understandable format.
5. **Section 1(3)(e)** – range of options. This emphasises that a "one solution" approach must not be adopted. The options in each case must be identified and considered. This could be from taking no action to making a CTO application.
6. **Section 1(3)(f)** – maximum benefit. The functions should not be discharged for reasons of convenience or concern for others but for the patient's maximum benefit.
7. **Section 1(3)(h)** – non-discrimination. The patient with a mental disorder should, wherever possible, retain the same rights and entitlements as those with other health needs.
8. **Section 1(4)** – minimum restriction. The patient should be provided with any necessary care, treatment and support in the least invasive manner and in the least restrictive manner and environment compatible with the delivery of safe and effective care, taking account of, where appropriate, the safety of others.
9. **Section 1(6)** – provision of appropriate services. Where an individual is obliged, because of compulsory measures, to comply with a programme of treatment or care, a parallel obligation is imposed on the health and social care authorities to provide safe and appropriate services, including ongoing care following discharge from compulsion. This applies to any person "who is, or has been, subject to compulsory powers under the Act".

The common term used for this principle is "reciprocity" borrowed from the Millan Report but the legal interpretation is more circumspect, that is, anyone discharging a function under the Act *"shall have regard to the importance of the provision of appropriate services."* In other words there is no automatic legal right to services.

10. **Section 3** - equal opportunities. All powers under the Act should be exercised without any direct or indirect discrimination on the grounds of physical disability, age, gender, sexual orientation, language, religion or national, ethnic or social origin.

Application of principles to patients under aged 18 years [section 2].

The Act introduced the fundamental principle of welfare where any application of the above ten principles must be interpreted in terms of the patient's welfare. This recognises the vulnerability of a young person within a system mainly designed for adults.

4) Specific professional roles in the Act

The Act defines some special professional roles to which a person must be appointed by the relevant body before they can discharge certain key functions under the Act:

i) **Mental Health Officer**

An MHO is a Social Worker who has more than two years post-qualifying experience and who has passed a nationally recognised course. Each local authority appoints their MHOs. In the case where local authorities share an out-of-hours service, the terms of employment are usually from the local authority coordinating the service. The MHO appointment should be renewed every five years. The statutory elements of the work of an MHO are:

- Providing an opinion on whether an individual requires either a hospital or community-based CTO or whether there are viable alternatives.

- Applying to the Tribunal for a CTO. This can only be done by an MHO.
- Ensuring that anyone subject to compulsory orders has access to advocacy services. The MHO must also inform the patient and their named person of their right to oppose the initial application, and of their right to appeal decisions made after the application is granted.
- Providing information on civil powers and their safeguards, for example, named persons, advance statements, although the 2003 Act states the hospital managers have this responsibility.[12]
- Preparing social circumstances reports on people who are compulsorily detained for more than 72 hours.
- There will be a designated MHO allocated to any person detained beyond 72 hours. They will have a role in overseeing any care services related to community-based compulsory treatment orders.

ii) **Doctor**

Any registered medical practitioner can grant a 72-hour emergency detention certificate. This may include a General Practitioner and all types of hospital practitioners working in any hospital, for example, general, psychiatric or learning disability hospitals.

iii) **Consultant Psychiatrist**

Called an "approved medical practitioner" in the Act, they are employed and registered by their Health Board or the State Hospital for Scotland under section 22 of the Act which then allows them to complete 28-day short-term detention certificates and to assess for all the orders in the Act.[13] This registration can also apply to other grades in psychiatry.

iv) **Specialist Registrar**

A doctor who has specialised training in psychiatry but below consultant status, that is, no supervision of staff. This also applies to Associate Specialists. They can be appointed as Approved Medical Practitioners (AMPs).

v) **Responsible medical officer**

An RMO is an AMP designated by the hospital manager to treat a detained patient.[14] They have extensive legal duties particularly in relation to reviewing compulsion orders.[15]

vi) **Designated medical practitioner**

These are "second opinion" AMPs appointed by the Mental Welfare Commission under Part 16, section 233 of the Act.

vii) **Nurses of a 'prescribed class'**

They can hold people in the ward for up to three hours for a medical examination.

5) Emergency detention certificate [Section 36]

◆ What is it?

This is a certificate formally detaining a person from either the community or already in any kind of hospital, for assessment. It applies where a medical practitioner believes a person is likely to have a mental disorder. The consent of an MHO should also be sought, where practicable. There are no legal rights of appeal hence why it should be used mainly for urgent admissions and solely for the purpose of urgent assessment.

The certificate gives no right to administer any treatment for a mental disorder except under specific urgent conditions, that is, saving life or where there is no likelihood of irreversible physical or psychological consequences. These conditions are listed in section 243 of the Act. With other non-urgent treatment, the practitioner has to seek patient consent. Where the patient does not have capacity to give consent, they have to complete a separate 'certificate of consent' using section 47 of the Adults with Incapacity (Scotland) Act 2000. This parallel legislation would then allow the practitioner to treat the detained patient for physical as well as mental disorders.

The legal criteria to be fulfilled are as follows:[(D)] [section 36(4) & (5)]

i) The person has a mental disorder which causes their decision-making to be 'significantly impaired'. Mental disorder is defined as mental illness; personality disorder; or learning disability, however caused or manifested;[16]
ii) It is necessary, as a matter of urgency, to detain the person for assessment;
iii) The person's health, safety or welfare, or the safety of another person, would be at significant risk if he or she were not detained; and
iv) Making arrangements for the possible granting of a short-term detention certificate would involve 'undesirable delay' (see below).

◆ Duration

The maximum period is 72 hours although this should be as short as possible to allow a specialist doctor in psychiatry to assess the patient as to whether to continue the certificate to allow for further assessment; discharge the patient or consider a short-term detention. The emphasis is on the specialist assessment, more so than a speedy transfer to a longer detention.[17]

◆ Requirements and procedures

Any registered medical practitioner can grant a certificate. Consent of an MHO should be sought where practicable.

- The medical practitioner must seek the consent of an MHO unless this is impracticable.[18]
- When a person is detained under the Act, the hospital manager must advise the nearest relative or whoever is living with the patient; also the named person (if known) and the Mental Welfare Commission of the admission.[19]

◆ Professionals involved

- Medical Practitioner (usually the person's General Practitioner, or if in hospital, a Senior House Officer when working, say, after 5pm).
- AMP.
- MHO.

◆ Persons notified

- Person's Nearest Relative – but only if they are living with the person.
- Any person who lives with the patient; named person (if known).
- Mental Welfare Commission.

Note: There are no formally prescribed forms for this certificate but the Scottish Executive has issued standardised forms, which should ensure the details, and criteria are done competently. See below for a reference to websites that list the mental health forms.

6) Short-Term detention certificate [Section 44]

◆ What is it?

This is a certificate formally detaining a person in a hospital for assessment and medical treatment. It is the preferred means of detention, as a specialist in Psychiatry is involved in the detention, and consent from an MHO has to be given. There are also legal rights of appeal to the Tribunal, unlike the emergency detention certificate.

◆ Duration

When the certificate is signed, the medical practitioner has 72 hours to admit the patient. The certificate then lasts for up to 28 days. The timescale is calculated as the day the patient is admitted plus 27 days. Any AMP can revoke (that is, stop) the certificate at any time. In practice, this would usually be the patient's RMO.

◆ Requirements and procedures

- Only an AMP can grant this certificate, with consent from an MHO.
- A short-term detention certificate can be used to admit or detain someone already in hospital or living in the community without using an emergency certificate.
- If the person is detained under an emergency certificate this is immediately revoked after a short-term detention certificate is granted.[20]
- The certificate has authority to assess and also give medical treatment to a patient.
- The criteria for admission are as follows.[21]

The AMP must consider it "likely" that:

i) the person has a mental disorder which causes their decision-making to be significantly impaired;
ii) it is necessary to detain the person for assessment or treatment;
iii) the person's health, safety or welfare, or the safety of another person, would be at significant risk if the person was not detained; and
iv) the granting of a short-term detention certificate is necessary (that is, the patient cannot be treated voluntarily).

- To grant a certificate, the AMP must consult and gain the consent of an MHO. The MHO can only give consent if the above criteria are met.
- If this is the first time the person has been detained the local authority has to appoint a designated MHO to complete a social circumstances report. This report has to be completed within 21 days of the start of the detention and will be submitted to the RMO and the Mental Welfare Commission.

- When the person is detained, the hospital manager must:

i) notify various parties of the detention, including the patient, the patient's named person, any guardian or welfare attorney, the Mental Welfare Commission and the Mental Health Tribunal;
ii) appoint an AMP to act as the patient's RMO.

- One of the RMO's duties is to keep the need for detention under review. If they consider the criteria above are no longer met, the certificate must be cancelled. It is good practice for the RMO to consult with the MHO when reviewing a certificate although there is no legal requirement to do so. The RMO is only required to give notice to the patient and other relevant parties after the revocation.[22]

- A patient or the patient's named person can appeal to the Tribunal against this certificate. The appeal can be wide-ranging and cover any aspect of the detention, for example, medical treatment issues as opposed to detention issues. The Tribunal is not legally obliged to meet specific timescales for appeals although the general practice is two weeks from the date of the appeal, assuming it is within the 28-day detention period.[23]

◆ Professionals involved

- An AMP (usually a Consultant Psychiatrist or a Senior Registrar).
- MHO.

◆ Persons notified

- Ward staff.
- Patient.
- Named person, if known.
- Guardian of the patient.
- Welfare attorney of the patient.
- Tribunal.
- Mental Welfare Commission.

7) Further Detention – extension of a short-term detention [Section 47]

◆ What is it?

This is a further period of detention added onto a short-term detention when a patient's condition deteriorates and there is not enough time for the MHO to apply for a CTO.

◆ Duration

Three working days maximum. Weekends and Scottish bank holidays are excluded.[E]

◆ Who can grant this?

The approved medical practitioner. They must try and get consent from any MHO if practicable.[F]

◆ Persons notified

The AMP must notify the following parties:

- the patient;
- the patient's named persons;
- the Tribunal;
- the Mental Welfare Commission;
- any guardian of the patient;
- any welfare attorney of the patient;
- MHO.

8) Compulsory treatment order [Section 57]

◆ What is it?

This is an order granted only by a Tribunal to compel a patient to receive care and treatment either in hospital or in the community. There are eight measures open to the Tribunal. Hospital and community measures cannot be included in the same order.

◆ Duration

This lasts initially for six months and can be extended by the patient's RMO, initially for a further six months and annually thereafter for up to two years. Beyond this period the Tribunal must be involved in a review.[(G)]

◆ Requirements and procedures

- Only the Tribunal can grant the order.
- Only an MHO can apply.
- The MHO has 14 days from the date of the last medical examination to submit the application to the Tribunal.
- The application has three components:

> i) Two mental health reports, one from the patient's General Practitioner[(H)] and one from an AMP, or two reports from two separate AMPs.[(I)]
> ii) An MHO report covering the MHO's views on the two medical reports, contents of any advance statement and the person's personal circumstances.
> iii) A Proposed Care Plan by the MHO in consultation with relevant professionals outlining the person's needs and also any care and treatment services required.

- The application form includes all the MHO duties. There are additional pages for the Tribunal to record their decision.

- After the Tribunal receives the application form they must notify the relevant parties and convene a hearing. The parties would then notify their witnesses.
- The Tribunal panel consists of three members – a legal member called a "Convener" who chairs the hearing; a general member (lay person); a medical member (a Psychiatrist usually at Consultant grade).
- They will use the following criteria to reach a decision. They must all be met for an order to be granted.[24]

i) the patient has a mental disorder;
ii) medical treatment is available which would be likely to prevent the disorder worsening, or would be likely to alleviate the symptoms or effects of the disorder;
iii) there would be a significant risk to the patient or to any other person if the patient was not provided with such treatment;
iv) the patient's ability to make decisions about the provision of medical treatment is significantly impaired because of their mental disorder;
v) the making of the compulsory treatment order is necessary.

Note: The general test is of "satisfaction"[25] which accounts for the individuality of Tribunal decisions. For example, a Tribunal may agree on the first four legal tests but are still not satisfied the order is necessary.

- The Tribunal has to consider an alternative, shorter, order called an interim compulsory treatment order [ICTO] where a patient is already detained under a section 44, short-term detention certificate.[26] This can last up to 28 days and can be extended to not more than a total of 56 days. This may be used by the Tribunal to allow time for more information where the Tribunal is unable to fully determine the application.
- An MHO or any interested party can also request in writing for an ICTO after the CTO application is lodged. This could be on the grounds of requesting more time to prepare evidence.
- An ICTO would still require a hearing and the same tests as for a CTO

would have to be met. The MHO therefore has to ensure the initial application is at least complete enough to allow an ICTO to be granted.

◆ Powers of the Tribunal – 8 measures[27]

- The Tribunal can grant 8 measures in any CTO as follows:

i) to be detained in a hospital;
ii) to have treatment in a hospital or in the community;
iii) to require a patient to attend a place for medical treatment;
iv) to require the patient to attend for community care services;
v) to require the patient to reside at a specified place;
vi) to allow the MHO and/or medical professional to visit;
vii) to require the patient to obtain the approval from the MHO of any proposed change of address;
viii) to require the patient to inform the MHO when moving to another address.

- The CTO can include 'recorded matters' which the Tribunal consider essential to making the order work. This can include care provider services or any form of community/health care service. These services however must be available in the first place.[(J)]
- The term "medical treatment" is defined as nursing; care; psychological intervention; habilitation (including education, and training in work, social and independent living skills); and rehabilitation.[28]
- There are different levels of treatment that require a second medical opinion before they can take place. This includes surgical operations; electro-convulsive therapy; treatments over a period of time. A person's treatment using medication has to be reviewed by a second medical opinion two months after it begins. The timing is therefore not necessarily from the beginning of the CTO itself. The patient's RMO may want further assessment before finally deciding on long-term medication.

Reviews [Sections 77-111]

- The patient's RMO can revoke [cancel] a CTO or an ICTO at any time if the criteria set out above are no longer met.[29]
- The CTO has to be formally reviewed by the RMO twice in the first year, at the six month stage and then annually. This would be the opportunity for the RMO to extend and also vary the order, that is, to remove or include other measures.[30]
- The CTO has to be reviewed by the Tribunal at least every two years if it hasn't been reviewed before this time. The timescale for review begins when the original order was granted by the Tribunal, for example, it might have started out as a hospital-based order then varied to community-based.
- The RMO can extend a CTO but only with MHO consent.[31] If the MHO disagrees with the RMO's determination to extend the CTO then the Tribunal must hold a hearing to review that determination to allow the MHO's views to be heard.[32]
- The Tribunal can grant an extension if the RMO also wants to include variations to the original CTO. This must be done in consultation with the patient/named person and relevant professionals, including the MHO.[33]
- The RMO must also review the CTO 'from time to time' [section 93(2)] and consider varying the powers in the CTO. The RMO would have no powers to extend the CTO as this review can only be done before the beginning of the mandatory reviews, that is, before the two monthly expiry period of a CTO.[34]

Non-compliance with the CTO [Section 112-114]

- If the patient fails to attend for the medical treatment measure only,[35] they can be brought to the place they normally receive the treatment or to any hospital for up to six hours[36]. The MHO has to give consent before this can take place[37].
- If any of the other measures in the CTO are breached, the patient can be brought to a hospital for up to 72 hours[38] and thereafter continue for 28 days[39]. MHO consent is only required for the 28 days period[40].

This period would allow the RMO to consider extending or varying the terms of the order before a Tribunal[K] [see Reviews above].

- If a patient refuses access and refuses to return to hospital when at home then a warrant to enter premises to return a patient can be granted by either a sheriff or a justice of the peace to return them to hospital[41]. The MHO can be involved in this removal but does not necessarily need to be the applicant. This is because the patient is already subject to an order through the Tribunal so any person authorised to return the patient, for example, a community psychiatric nurse (CPN) or an registered mental nurse (RMN) can apply for a warrant[42].

Suspensions [Section 127 and Section 128]

- A CTO or an ICTO can be suspended for periods of up to six months at a time if the patient is in hospital. The hospital-based suspension cannot last for more than a total of nine months.[43]
- A community-based CTO can only be suspended for up to three months[44]. A community-based Interim CTO cannot be suspended presumably because of the limited duration of this order.

9) Nurses holding power [Section 299]

- This is the formal authority for an RMN to stop a voluntary patient leaving hospital prior to medical examination.[L]
- It can last up to three hours. The first two hours are to arrange for a medical assessment and the last hour for the assessment to take place. The last hour begins when the medical practitioner arrives to begin their assessment. The MHO should be informed of the detention as soon as possible.
- The person must already have been in hospital on an informal basis and receiving treatment for a mental disorder.
- The nurse using this power must be qualified and registered in mental illness or learning disability. The nurse must assess the patient as needing to be detained in hospital to protect their health, safety or

welfare and that a medical examination is necessary. The patient will therefore usually be accommodated in a specialist hospital for either mental illness or learning disability.

- A patient detained on this basis cannot be detained again immediately under this power when it expires. They must either be formally detained under an emergency or a short-term detention certificate or remain in hospital on a voluntary (informal) basis.

◆ Professionals involved

- Nursing Staff registered in Mental Health Nursing and/or Learning Disability. This effectively means any nurse who is so registered, regardless of staff grading.
- Any medical practitioner: Senior House Officer, Senior Registrar or a Consultant Psychiatrist, Mental Health Officer.

◆ Persons notified

- Hospital Manager.
- Mental Welfare Commission.
- MHO.

10) Inquiries and powers of entry [Section 35, Section 292 & 293]

There are two types of orders:

1. Inquiries involving three separate warrants; and
2. Removal orders involving two kinds of warrants.

Note: The person subject to the warrant must be 16 years of age or over.

1. Inquiries [Section 35]

The warrants available under this section are:

i) to allow entry to lockfast premises;
ii) to allow a medical examination for up to three hours;
iii) to allow access to medical records where the person is unable to give consent.

- They can be applied for collectively or separately, depending on the circumstances.
- The set criteria for granting these warrants are that it appears to the local authority that the person has a mental disorder and as a result, is exposed to ill-treatment or neglect; or is unable to look after him or herself or their property/financial affairs; may be living alone without care and unable to look after him or herself or property or financial affairs; is likely to suffer significant harm if not removed to a place of safety.
- The MHO must specify the names of, say, medical professionals who may accompany him. The police constable(s) do not have to be named.
- The warrant can last up to 8 days to allow the MHO time to arrange the assessment.[45]
- The expectation is the medical assessment would lead to either an emergency detention certificate or a short-term detention certificate.
- The warrants themselves do not allow the person to be removed. If the person is not formally detained using either an emergency or a short-term detention certificate, then a removal order can be used where appropriate.
- There are statutory forms that must be used by the MHO for each warrant.[46]

2. Entry to premises and removal order [Section 292 & Section 293]

- These separate warrants can be used to remove a 'patient' already subject to an order under the Act [section 292], or to remove a 'person' who has a mental disorder but who is not detained under the Act, from their premises if refused access [section 293].
- Section 292 allows an authorised person such as a nurse; an MHO or any police constable to apply for a warrant for a person already detained. The application will be either to a sheriff or a justice of the peace.
- The authorised person, MHO or police constable who has this warrant can have a medical practitioner or any authorised person, for example, a nurse, with them to carry out the warrant. The subject of

the warrant can be removed to any place, for example, to a hospital or a residence specified in the original order.

- There is no timescale to exercise the warrant nor is there a right of appeal.
- Section 293 allows the removal of a person who has already been assessed as having a mental disorder. The set criteria is the person is exposed to ill-treatment or neglect; or is unable to look after him or herself or their property/financial affairs; is living alone without care and unable to look after himself or property or financial affairs; is likely to suffer significant harm if not removed to a place of safety.
- Only the MHO can apply for this warrant.
- The MHO must specify the names of, say, medical/nursing people who may accompany him. The police constable does not have to be named.
- The person and any interested party such as the person's named person or primary carer can appeal to the sheriff before the removal order is granted. The court has to notify these persons of the application. The MHO can request that the sheriff dispense with this notification if he considers it would be prejudicial to the person's welfare if they were present at the hearing.
- Once granted, the warrant has to be used within 72 hours and a police constable(s) can open lockfast premises and hold that person in a place of safety for up to seven days. This would usually be in a hospital for further medical assessment.
- If a justice of the peace signs the warrant, there is no right of appeal by the person or any other relevant party.
- There are statutory forms, which must be used by the nurse and/or MHO for each warrant.[47]

Note: See Chapter 6 for guidance on warrants.

11) Police Powers [Section 297]

- The Act authorises the police to remove from a public place to a "place of safety" any person who appears to be suffering from a mental disorder and to be in need of immediate care or treatment or to protect either the individual or other people.
- If detained they can be held for up to 24 hours to allow for a psychiatric assessment and for any care or treatment arrangements to be made.
- A place of safety is defined as the local hospital Accident & Emergency Unit. A police station is not regarded as a place of safety. The Act makes it clear this should only be used if no other place of safety is immediately available.[48]
- The next stage would be for the person to be examined in the place of safety by a medical practitioner to rule out physical causes of the suspected mental disorder and then transfer the patient to an appropriate ward.
- The police would be expected to remain with the person until a medical assessment is complete and a decision is made.
- If the person is assessed as being mentally ill then an MHO would be involved to assess whether or not to give consent to either an emergency or a short-term detention.
- The police are obliged to contact the person's nearest relative and/or anyone who lives with or cares for the person, whether by contract or voluntarily.
- The police must also inform the Mental Welfare Commission within 14 days of the removal.

◆ Professionals involved

- Police Constable.
- Psychiatrist or Senior House Officer.
- MHO.

12) Safeguards and rights of review and appeal[49]

The Act provides additional rights for people accessing mental health services and increased safeguards as follows:

- it puts a duty on local authorities to undertake an **assessment of needs** where certain conditions are met and gives patients, carers and named persons the right to request an assessment of needs from the local authority or NHS Board;
- it gives all detained people with a mental disorder the right of access to **independent advocacy services** and puts a duty on NHS Boards and local authorities to ensure the availability and accessibility of advocacy services;
- any person over the age of 16 can nominate a **named person** (an adult over 16 years) who has the right to be kept informed of the patient's status in certain circumstances set out in the Act and may act on behalf of the patient, including making applications and appeals to the Tribunal. If there is no named person then this role would then default to an unpaid primary carer or lastly to a nearest relative. The MHO can apply to the Tribunal to nominate a named person if he/she thinks a nominated named person is inappropriate;
- any person, including a child of any age can make an **advance statement** regarding how they would wish to be treated or not treated in the event of being formally detained. This can be done by anyone even if they have not been mentally ill. The main condition is they have to have mental capacity at the time of making the statement. This statement verifying capacity has to be witnessed by a prescribed person, termed the "witness", such as a doctor, nurse, social worker, clinical psychologist, solicitor;
- any **informal patient**, that is, a patient, who is not held in hospital under a CTO, or others on their behalf, including an MHO, can apply to the Tribunal for an order requiring hospital managers to release the patient. The Tribunal must first be satisfied the patient is being unlawfully detained [section 291, p. 213].
- it provides a framework of safeguards for different kinds of **medical treatment**, including neurosurgery for mental disorder and electro-convulsive therapy;

- any patient, or someone acting on their behalf, has the **right of appeal** to the Tribunal against detention where they consider they are being detained in conditions of **excessive security**. They could be detained either in the State Hospital, Carstairs or in a locked ward in their own local hospital. The right of appeal for State Hospital patients started from 1 May 2006. The appeal date for people detained in other hospitals is still to be determined.[50]

13) Mentally disordered offenders – summary

◆ Background to new provisions

- The Act substantially reforms the law relating to people with mental disorder who enter the criminal justice system. This is dealt with in Parts 8 to 13.
- Part 8 amends the Criminal Procedure (Scotland) Act 1995 ('1995 Act'), to give courts new options on how they deal with people with mental disorder. It provides new orders that a court may make:

Assessment order
This can last for up to 28 days.

Treatment order
This can last until the person is sentenced.

Interim compulsion order
This is normally 12 weeks or less but can, unusually, be extended for up to one year.

Compulsion order
This initially lasts for six months.

- A court will still be able to make:

A transfer for treatment/hospital direction
– hospital treatment and/or prison sentence.

A restriction order
(in combination with a compulsion order).

- Part 8 also keeps Scottish Ministers' powers to transfer a prisoner to hospital for treatment of a mental disorder, and introduces the transfer for treatment direction.
- Parts 9 to 13 of the Act set out how some of these new orders will be reviewed once they are made, and describe procedures for the transfer of patients and the suspension of detention of patients who are subject to certain orders.

14) Legislation repealed/amended by the Act

The Act has amended or repealed several major Scottish Acts.

Among the most affected are:

The Mental Health (Scotland) Act 1984
– whole 1984 Act repealed.
The Mental Health (Detention) (Scotland) Act 1991
– whole 1991 Act repealed.
Mental Health (Patients in the Community) Act 1995
Community Care Orders. Sections 4-6 repealed.
The Criminal Procedure (Scotland) Act 1995
– amended.
The Adults with Incapacity (Scotland) Act 2000
– amended.

Note: See Schedule 5 in the Act for the full list of repeals and amendments.

Further reading/website references:

Legislative context

The most commonly used legislation and policy are summarised in the following list:

Adult Support & Protection Act 2007 – partially implemented from April 2007.
Adults with Incapacity (Scotland) Act 2000.
Care Programme Approach guidance 1996.
Care in the Community (Direct Payments) Act 1996.
Carers Recognition (Scotland) Act 1995.
Children (Scotland) Act 1995.
Chronically Sick and Disabled Persons Act 1970.
Code of Practice Mental Health (Care and Treatment) (Scotland) Act 2003.
Community Care and Health (Scotland) Act 2002.
Criminal Procedures (Scotland) Act 1995.
A Framework for Mental Health Services in Scotland 1997.
Mental Health (Care and Treatment) (Scotland) Act 2003.
National Assistance Act 1948.
National Health Service and Community Care Act 1990.
Regulation of Care (Scotland) Act 2001.
Restricted Patients Scottish Office Guidance 1993.
Sexual Offenders Act 1997.
Social Work (Scotland) Act 1968.
Websites:

i) The Act, Regulations: www.opsi.gov.uk/legislation
ii) Code of Practice: www.scotland.gov.uk/publications

Useful contacts:

Mental Welfare Commission: Tel. 0131 222 6111
Mental Health Tribunal for Scotland: Tel. 01698 390000

Footnotes:

1 section 328(1).
2 section 274(4).
3 section 278.
4 This material is taken from a useful publication by the Mental Welfare Commission – *An Introduction to the Mental Health (Care and Treatment) (Scotland) Act 2003* website: www.mwcscot.org.uk (see under Publications).
5 Chaired by Rt. Hon Bruce Millan (b. 1927), a Labour Member of Parliament, Glasgow (1959-88); a former Scottish Secretary (1976-79) and European Commissioner (1988-95). He was commissioned by Sam Galbraith, Scottish Health Secretary in 1999 to review mental health law in Scotland. The Millan Committee report New Directions (2001) largely influenced the shape of the 2003 Act. All tribunal hearing centres are termed "The Millan suite" to acknowledge this achievement.
6 For a fuller discussion on the Millan Committee and their influence on the shape of the Act, see Atkinson, J. (2006) Private and Public Protection: Civil Mental Health Legislation, Dunedin Academic Press.
7 Separate powers for criminal proceedings are discussed in Chapter 5.
8 section 65; also section 69(a) where a short-term certificate has previously been granted.
9 See Appendix 1 for more detail on this power.
10 See Franks, R.A. and Cobb, D. (2005) Mental Health (Care and Treatment) (Scotland) Act 2003, Edinburgh: W. Green for fuller discussion of these principles as they correspond to the Millan Committee report in General Notes p.19.
11 sections 1-3.
12 section 260(5)(a).
13 These orders are listed in CoP, vol, chapter 9, par 01, p 132.
14 section 230.
15 see CoP, vol 1, chapter 9, paras 02 p 133 for details of this role.
16 section 328(1).
17 CoP, vol 2, chapter 7, para 07, p.183.
18 section 36(3)(d); section 36(6).
19 section 38(4).
20 section 55.
21 section 44(4) see footnote 30, p.10 for detail.
22 section 49(3); CoP, vol 2, chapter 2; paras 68-71, pp.41-42.
23 CoP, vol 2, chapter 2; paras 72 - 75, pp. 42-43.
24 section 64(5).
25 section 64(4)(a).
26 section 69(a).
27 section 66(1).
28 section 329(1).
29 section 79(2) This applies to all the mandatory reviews , that is, 6 month and annual reviews.
30 section 77(3). The RMO can ask another AMP to complete this review, for example, Registrar.
31 section 86. This is called "making a determination" to the Tribunal who ultimately grant the extension.
32 section 101(2)(a)(ii) The MHO has to carry out a range of duties under section 85 before reaching a decision. This work would be part of their evidence (see

Chapter 4 for detail).
33 sections 88 and 91.
34 section 93.
35 section 66(1)(c).
36 section 112(1)
37 section 112 (2)
38 section 113(5)
39 section 114(2)
40 section 114(3)
41 section 292(1)
42 section 292(5)
43 section 127(1) applies to CTOs; section 127(3) applies to interim CTOs – with no time limits as the Tribunal determines the detention period for up to 56 days.
44 section 128(1)
45 section 35(2)(a). The warrant cannot be used more than once to gain entry during this 8-day period.
46 See Mental Welfare Commission for Scotland website at www.mwcscot.org.uk which includes "New Forms".
47 See Mental Welfare Commission for Scotland website at www.mwcscot.org.uk which includes "New Forms".
48 section 297(5).
49 Mental Welfare Commission have a list of publications on some of these safeguards. Website: www.mwcscot.org.uk which includes Publications.
50 sections 264 & 265 to 267.

Endnotes:

(A) The Code of Practice suggests where a person is immediately at risk, and then a "pragmatic approach" would be for the first practitioner to come into contact with the patient to grant the certificate. The Act also takes account of this in terms of there being an "undesirable delay" if an approved medical practitioner is not available. This can be abused, especially out-of-hours. [CoP, vol 2, chapter 7, para 12, p.184; section 36(5)(c)].

(B) The practitioner however has to justify why they decided not to consult or seek MHO consent in the certificate. It is likely the practitioner will at least try and seek MHO consent. If they consult and the MHO is unable to attend, the Code of Practice suggests the MHO visit the detained patient shortly after, even though formal consent has not been given. The Code also allows an MHO to consent if they have close knowledge of the patient and their recent history; or have seen the patient within 72 hours of giving consent. [CoP, vol 2, chapter 7, paras 43, 44, p.195].

(C) The legal status conferred on an AMP relates to section 22 of the Act , that is, where they are approved by their Health Boards and have undergone further training in the use of the 2003 Act. Other grades of Psychiatrists can therefore be accredited as AMPs using this section, for example, Registrars.

(D) Note. These legal tests are based on "likelihood" the patient requires up to 72 hours detention. This takes into account the non-specialist status of the medical practitioner and also the certificate is not appealable. Only an AMP can revoke it. The same likelihood test applies for short-term certificates which can however be appealed by the patient and named person using the Tribunal system.

(E) Section 47(8)(c). There are 8 Scottish bank holidays/annum. They are published from 2004-2010 and available on the internet under "Scottish bank holidays". The Tribunal does not recognise any of the local authority Public Holidays such as Easter Monday.

(F) Section 47(3)(c)(i), also section 47(6). Given the deterioration in the patient's mental state, the patient's RMO and designated MHO may not be available, hence why the 2003 Act recognises an AMP/any MHO can be involved in this assessment, for example, out-of-hours or at weekends. The AMP has discretion to sign the certificate if it is impracticable to consult or seek consent from an MHO. The patient's designated MHO would then be involved in applying for a CTO.

(G) Tribunal reviews only applied to restricted patients detained under section 189(2)(b) in criminal proceedings from October 2006. The Scottish Government implemented civil compulsory power reviews (s.101(2)(b)) and other criminal proceeding (s.165(2)(b)) from October 2007.

(H) Section 58(4). The Act recognises the patient's GP "may" [quote] complete the second medical examination although the implication is there has to be good reason. The Code of Practice on the other hand interprets having a GP involved as a best practice issue , that is, pre-existing relationship with more extensive patient history not necessarily available to the RMO. The GP too would be helpful where community-based CTO measures are being sought as they would have a key part to play in the implementation. Otherwise, the 2003 Act recognises the legal value of two independent specialists reports. [CoP, vol 2, chapter 3, para 11, p.63]

(I) Section 58(2)(a). It cannot be assumed the patient already has an RMO if not detained under section 44. The Code of Practice however suggests it would be good practice for the first mental health report to be completed by the patient's RMO. This distinction between an AMP and an RMO is only recognised in Form DET 2, page 6 where the AMP has to state whether or not the patient can instruct a solicitor. The guidance notes state "it would be best practice for the patient's RMO to complete this section" [sections 58(2) & s.57(5)(c); CoP, vol 2, chapter 3, para 11 , p.63 & para 34, p.71].

(J) Section 64(4)(ii) & 64(5)(b). The legal test for a Tribunal to decide on recorded matters is their "appropriateness" to the detained patient's care and treatment. The underlying principle applied by the Tribunal with recorded matters is "provision of appropriate services" under section 1(6). Examples could be a specific resource or directing the frequency of a care professional's time with a patient. They are then listed in Part 5b of the Form CTO 1.

The Code of Practice uses the term "essential to the care package"" in describing the reasons for having recorded matters. It may be prudent for the MHO as applicant to make it clear at the tribunal hearing what resources are available to make any recorded matter feasible. The MHO should not feel under pressure to accept any inappropriate or non-essential recorded matters if they are either not feasible or unavailable. A recorded matter can only be reviewed by the Tribunal through an application by the patient's RMO under section 96 if this is not met. To avoid this further legal action, the MHO may for example, consider requesting a brief interim CTO using section 65(2) if this knowledge is not to hand at the Tribunal.

(K) Section 113 applies to the 72-hour detention. There is no timescale to return a patient to hospital as they are already formally detained under a CTO. The patient can be taken to any hospital, not necessarily where the RMO is based. Section 114 applies to the 28-day detention. These detentions run consecutively, that is, 72 hours + 28 days. The 72-hour detention is related to non-compliance. The 28-day detention is a review of the CTO and implies there will be an application to the Tribunal, by the RMO and not the MHO, to vary or modify the measures.

(L) 55 Section 299(1)(a) also includes people on probation under section 228 of the 1995 Act and who are required to receive treatment in a hospital, whether as in-patients or out-patients. The probation order is an agreement and an alternative to a sentence therefore the patient would be regarded as informal.

Chapter 2

Emergency and Short-term Detention Certificates

1) Introduction

Summary points common to both certificates

- The Act allows for any medical practitioner to detain a patient using an emergency detention certificate (EDC) but only an approved medical practitioner (AMP) with specialist training in Psychiatry can detain a patient using a short-term detention certificate[1].
- The MHO has to consent to both emergency and short-term detention certificates for a patient to either be admitted or detained in hospital. These certificates can be used when a person is staying either in the community or already in hospital.
- There is some discretion for a medical practitioner to dispense with MHO consent with regard to an EDC but they must record what steps were taken to contact an MHO. There is no discretion for an AMP when considering a short-term detention certificate.
- An MHO signature is now included in the new Forms being issued from late 2007.
- The Code of Practice states it would not be good practice for an AMP to "shop around" for an MHO to give consent where the first MHO has already refused consent. If there is a second MHO opinion sought then the reasons for the first MHO refusing consent should be made clear in advance of the second MHO assessment.[2]
- An MHO usually cannot give consent unless they see the patient in person. Prior to giving consent, the MHO should see the patient and have a discussion with the medical practitioner about the legal tests for admission. These tests are based on the likelihood that the person needs to be detained[3] (see below for details).

- In the short-term detention certificate, the MHO may, if they have time before giving consent, identify the patient's named person. The medical practitioner has to record and make a statement that they have discussed the detention with a patient's named person.[4]
- If the MHO is unable to perform these section 45 duties, they have a further seven days after giving consent to record the steps taken to fulfil those duties.[(A)]
- The Code of Practice gives a few examples where the MHO could give consent without interviewing the patient:[5]

    i) where communication difficulties with the patient cannot be overcome speedily;
    ii) where the patient is extremely dangerous or violent;
    iii) where the patient refuses to co-operate or participate in the interview.

- Where this is the case, the Code of Practice suggests the MHO elicit information about the proposed detention from other sources instead, for example, the patient's family, friends, doctor, CPN, advance statements, social work records.[6]
- The Code of Practice advises:

> *"It would be good practice for the MHO to ensure that he/she undertakes an assessment of the patient as soon as possible after the certificate has been granted and to make available to the hospital managers, the relevant local authority/authorities and the Mental Welfare Commission a full account of the exceptional circumstances which led to the MHO consenting to the certificate without interviewing the patient."*[7]

- The Code of Practice states the MHO must:

> *"make sure that as many forms of informal and less restrictive treatment as practicable have been explored before consenting to the last resort of a compulsory detention."*[8]

- The MHO has a role to secure the patient's premises and consider the needs of any dependants and pets. There is no direct reference to this in the 2003 Act but the Code of Practice cites the National Assistance Act 1948 as the legal source of this responsibility.[9]
- The National Standards for MHO Services states:

> *"Where an MHO assessment does not result in the use of compulsion or statutory measures, the MHO or another designated worker continues to assist the service user and their carers, as far as possible, in arranging the care they may be assessed as needing.*[10]

- The Code of Practice states that any hospital admission should be based on "*need alone*" regardless of whether the patient is subject to compulsory powers.[11]
- The medical practitioner, or the AMP in the case of a short-term detention certificate from the community, has three days to arrange a hospital admission after the certificate is signed. This certificate has to be passed to the hospital manager before a patient is formally admitted and the detention period begins. A ward-based nurse can represent the hospital manager.[12]

2) Application of CAN model to emergency detention certificate

◆ STAGE 1: Consultation

Who is asking the MHO? What is expected of the MHO?

Information points:

- The Code of Practice gives three examples where it may be impracticable for a medical practitioner to consult an MHO:

    i) there is immediate, serious or life-threatening danger to the patient and/or others around the patient, for example, violence or self-harm;

i) no MHO can be contacted;
iii) the patient is likely to abscond or has absconded immediately after the medical examination has taken place.[13]

Note: see references to The Act/Code of Practice in footnotes.

Practice points:

- The MHO can only give consent by telephone if they have either met the person to be detained or if they have close knowledge of the person and the person's recent history. The Code of Practice suggests the timescale when last seeing the person would be unlikely to be more than 48 to 72 hours prior to the detention.[14]
- Where telephone consent has been given, the MHO should attempt to see the patient as soon as possible after the certificate has been granted, or arrange for another MHO to do so.[15]
- The Act allows a minimum of four hours at any time from 8pm to 12 midnight on the day the assessment was completed for the Form DET 1 certificate to be signed. This should be sufficient time to consult an MHO.
- The practitioner has to state in the certificate what time the assessment began and was signed. This may be an academic point in practice given these are usually done very quickly, mainly due to the circumstances.[16]
- The timescale to admit the detained person to hospital is 72 hours from the exact time the certificate is signed by the medical practitioner.[17]
- After admission, the detained patient can then remain in hospital for up to 72 hours, calculated from the moment the person is admitted.[18]
- The certificate only authorises the patient to be detained in hospital for an assessment to allow a specialist in psychiatry to review this certificate. The legal test for admission is based on the "likelihood" the patient has a mental disorder.[19] The patient therefore has no legal right to receive treatment while under an emergency certificate unless the following conditions apply:[20]

i) The patient requires urgent treatment for the mental disorder. The four conditions are listed under section 243 of the Act.
ii) The patient consents to medical treatment – for a physical or a mental disorder, for example, diabetes/heart problems related to mental illness.
iii) The medical practitioner completes section 47 consent to medical treatment form under the 2000 Act, which allows treatment for both physical and mental illness.(B)
iv) In the case of a child, the consent of the child in terms of the Age of Legal Capacity (Scotland) Act 1991 and the Children (Scotland) Act 1995.

◆ STAGE 2: Assessment

■ ■ ■ Information points:

- The MHO must consider the criteria for emergency detention as listed in section 36(4) and section 36(5):

  i) likely to have a mental disorder [section 36(4)(a)];
  ii) ability to make decisions is significantly impaired [section 36(4)(b)];
  iii) it is a "matter of urgency" the patient be admitted [section 36(5)(a)];
  iv) there would be "significant risk" to the patient's health, safety or welfare; or the safety of any other person [section 36(5)(b)];
  v) alternative arrangements – short-term detention certificate – would involve an "undesirable delay" [section 36(5)(c)].

There are two searching questions outlined to support these last criteria, for example:

i) what efforts were made to the granting of a short-term detention certificate?
ii) why was informal/voluntary care not appropriate?

Practice points:

i) consent given:

- The MHO should complete a short follow-up account of their involvement and assessment to the patient's RMO and the medical practitioner who granted the certificate.[21]
- The National Standards for MHO Services also states:

> *"The outcome of MHO assessment is recorded in case files in accordance with agency policy and is communicated to the extent appropriate, within the bounds of confidentiality, to the service user, their named person, the medical practitioner, the person's nearest relative, the person's keyworker (where one exists), and, where relevant, proxies under the Adults with Incapacity (Scotland) 2000 Act."*[22]

ii) consent not given:

- If MHO consent is not given then the medical practitioner cannot sign the emergency detention certificate.
- If the MHO withholds consent, the Code of Practice lists the following actions. The MHO must ensure that:[23]
  a) A discussion takes place with the medical practitioner as to why consent was withheld and why alternatives were proposed, if preferable;
  b) There is a written record of the decision which the Code advises could then be given to the patient's GP, RMO and the Mental Welfare Commission;[24] where there is a viable and safe alternative to detention;
  c) The practical arrangements which will support this alternative are in place;
  d) Where relevant, others who are involved with the patient's care and treatment are aware of the alternatives and agree their role in any arrangements supporting it;
  e) There is a contingency plan in place should the alternative arrangements break down.

Note: see Appendix 2 for details on procedures before and after admission.

◆ STAGE 3: Notification by MHO

- The MHO should complete a short follow-up account of their involvement and assessment to the patient's RMO and the practitioner who granted the certificate.[25]

Note: see Chapter 9 for suggested standard letter to medical practitioner [Letter 1].

3) Key issues about duration of an emergency detention certificate

- The detained person cannot appeal the certificate.
- The Act states that an AMP should assess a detained person as soon as practicable to review the detention.[26]
- The important issue is not in reaching a decision on the first assessment. The emphasis should be that the detained patient is being monitored by a specialist in psychiatry who then has to make a final decision within 72 hours of that person's admission to either revoke or lapse the certificate after 72 hours or place them on a short-term detention certificate.[27]
- The Psychiatrist's assessment examines whether or not the person detained fulfils the conditions within the five criteria used for admission by a non-specialist.
- Another alternative is for the Psychiatrist to keep the patient on an EDC in order to satisfy them it is necessary for further detention. This could apply where a patient presents as suffering from drug/alcohol abuse or has no clear psychiatric symptoms, for example, mute. The Act only infers this positive approach.[28]
- The Psychiatrist has to complete a revocation form that lists one of the reasons for revoking the certificate as "*expiry of the authority to detain*". This explicitly means a person can still be detained for 72 hours [Form REV 1].

4) Application of CAN model to a short-term detention certificate

◆ STAGE 1: Consultation

Who is asking the MHO? What are they looking for?

Information points:

- The medical practitioner has to be registered under section 22 of the Act, that is, a doctor with specialist knowledge in mental disorders. This is usually a Consultant Psychiatrist but can also be an experienced Senior House Officer who has further qualifications in psychiatry or a Specialist Registrar in Psychiatry. In any case, the legal test remains the same, that is, further training and formal accreditation by the NHS Board employing them. The Act uses the term "approved medical practitioner" ("AMP") to make that distinction.[29]
- The AMP has to have MHO consent for the certificate to be valid. The AMP will have up to 72 hours after completing the assessment to contact an MHO and thereafter complete the 7-page certificate.[30]
- There are five legal tests that must be met before a certificate can be signed. The certificate has text boxes for completion in each test as follows:

  i) The patient has a mental disorder [section 44(4)(a)];
  ii) ability to make decisions about medical treatment is significantly impaired;[31]
  iii) it is necessary to detain the patient to assess and/or treat;[32]
  iv) there would be "*significant risk*" to the patient's health, safety or welfare; or the safety of any other person;[33]
  v) the granting of the certificate is necessary.[34]

Note: Page 2 of Form DET 2 words this in terms of the AMP "*I consider that it is likely the patient has the following type(s) of mental disorder.*" This allows for flexibility if diagnosis was uncertain. The conditions have the same flexibility of judgement as in the EDC that the relevant detention criteria are "*likely* "to be met.[35]

Practice points:

- An MHO has to give consent after seeing a patient in person and having discussion with the AMP about the legal tests for admission. This may also involve speaking to a person's carer.[36]
- The hospital manager or a ward-based representative has to complete Part 2, Form DET 2 which details the date of admission and the 28th day of detention, that is, the expiry date. The form states: "*unless revoked or extended this authorisation to detain will cease at midnight at the end of the 28th day*".[37]
- A practical way to calculate this maximum period is 1 + 27 days, that is, the day of admission, regardless of time when admitted, plus 27 days.

◆ STAGE 2: Assessment

Information points:

- The MHO has to carry out duties under section 45(1) before giving consent. If it is impracticable to perform these duties, the MHO then has another seven days to inform the AMP of their attempt to carry out the legal duties (see note (A) in endnotes for current changes).
- The MHO has to take into account the following issues as an initial step towards giving consent:[38]
  a) make sure the detention criteria have been fulfilled;
  b) the principles in the Act have been followed, for example, all relevant least restrictive alternatives have been considered;
  c) could the patient's treatment be provided on a voluntary basis?;
  d) is there sufficient information to make a sound judgement?
- MHO duties under section 45(1) are:
  i) interview the patient;
  iii) obtain the name and address of the patient's named person [see Chapter 7 for further details];
  iii) inform the patient of the availability of independent advocacy services; and take steps to ensure that the patient has the opportunity to make use of these advocacy services.

Practice points:

i) consent given:

- The MHO is required to sign the certificate on page 4.[(C)] The AMP must detail the name and address of the MHO.

ii) consent not given:

- If the MHO withholds consent, the Code of Practice lists actions the MHO must consider. These are the same as duties if the MHO refuses consent to an emergency certificate.[39]
- The Code of Practice also suggests an option to refusing consent might be for the MHO "*to encourage the practitioner to defer making a firm decision on the need to grant the certificate until the MHO has had the full opportunity to contribute to the joint assessment process*"[40]
- The AMP has up to 72 hours to complete and sign the certificate, allowing for this kind of debate.[41]

◆ STAGE 3: Notification by MHO

i) MHO Consent/non-consent to the detention

- The MHO should complete a short follow-up account of their involvement and assessment to the practitioner who granted the certificate and also the RMO allocated to the patient after the detention.[42]
- The National Standards for MHO Services states:

> a) "*The outcome of MHO assessments is recorded in case files in accordance with agency policy and is communicated to the extent appropriate, within the bounds of confidentiality, to the service user, their named person, the medical practitioner, the person's nearest relative, the person's keyworker (where one exists), and, where relevant, proxies under the Adults with Incapacity (Scotland) 2000 Act.*"[43]

> b) "*Where an MHO assessment does not result in the use of compulsion or statutory measures, the MHO or another designated worker continues to assist the service user and their carers, as far as possible, in arranging the care they may be assessed as needing.*[44]

ii) MHO unable to perform some or all of the section 45(1) duties.

- Given the AMP is unlikely to use the full 72 hours to complete a section 44 certificate, the MHO will probably not be able to fulfil all their legal duties as described above.
- The revised Form DET 2 form allows the MHO discretion to give their reasons for not fulfilling any of the three statutory duties of interviewing the patient, confirming the named person and informing the patient of their advocacy and appeal rights. Furthermore, the Form states "*by completing this form there is no longer a requirement to complete DET 3*" (text box 6, page 4).
- The MHO would still have to carry out unfinished duties within seven days of the certificate being signed (see (iii) and (iv) below for guidance).[45]

Note: see above for further guidance on the circumstances where an MHO can give consent without being able to interview the patient.

iii) MHO writes to advocacy services.[46]

- The MHO has to be proactive in making available advocacy services for a person about to be detained. This may be difficult to organise. The MHO should take more formal steps after the detention for example, a standard letter to Advocacy Services about the detention to allow them to make independent contact with the detained person.

Note: see Chapter 9 for suggested standard letter to Advocacy Services.

iv) MHO to ascertain the name and address of the named person.

- The named person can either be nominated by the person detained or be a default nomination if there is no formal nomination. If the detained patient has the capacity and agrees to either the primary carer or the nearest relative being the default named person, they need not make a formal nomination.
- The MHO has a duty to assess the appropriateness of any type of named person. This also applies to the default named persons of children, usually their parent.
- The MHO also has to make the named person aware of their responsibilities and give them the opportunity to withdraw their default or formal nomination.

Note: See Chapter 7 for guidance on named person.
See Chapter 9 for a standard letter to named person covering these situations.
See Chapter 8 for guidance on preparation of a social circumstances report.

5) Best practice points for MHO following detention

The Code of Practice lists 12 best practice points an MHO should consider after a person is detained.[47] They are:

1. Ensuring that the patient is as aware as is possible of his/her status and rights and has access to information on representation, advocacy services, and interpretation or translation services;
2. Consulting the patient's carers and eliciting their views;
3. Attending the ward assessment meeting and liaising with ward staff and other members of the multi-disciplinary team, particularly where the patient was using mental health services prior to being hospitalised;
4. Ensuring that ward medical staff are aware of the patient's views on consent to treatment, including the existence and content of any advance statement made by the patient;

5. Ensuring that a written record of the MHO decision to give consent is included in the patient's records;
6. Liaising with community care teams, other sections of the local authority (Criminal Justice Teams, Community Mental Health Team, Housing, Education, Leisure and Recreation, etc.) and other relevant statutory and non-statutory organisations (for example, supported accommodation or visiting support workers) for the purposes of through-care planning, wherever necessary;
7. Ensuring that any dependants which the patient might have are being appropriately cared for, particularly where there may be children or other vulnerable persons previously in the charge of the patient;
8. Securing the patient's property and belongings, if necessary, and arranging, for example, suitable pet care;
9. Determining whether a full community care assessment should be undertaken under section 227 of the Act and making such a request to the local authority if they are not going to be undertaking this assessment themselves;
10. Beginning preparations for any eventual CTO application or for a discharge plan of care;
11. Attending to issues which the patient may face in relation to their personal finances (for example, benefits, employment, etc.) because of their detention in hospital;
12. Making sure that the patient and the named person, etc., remain fully aware of their rights throughout the detention period – for example, in relation to their right to appeal for a revocation of the short-term detention certificate under section 50 or in relation to their rights to advocacy services.

Footnotes:

1 Forms are on the Mental Welfare Commission for Scotland website: www.mwcscot.org.uk (listed as "New Act Forms").
2 CoP, vol 2, chapter 2; para 30, p. 29.
3 CoP, vol 2, chapter 7, para 39,193.
4 section 44(10). See Chapter 7 on named person.
5 CoP, vol 2; chapter 2; para 42, p.32.

6 CoP, vol 2, chapter 2, para 43, p. 32 ; National Standards for MHOs, No.2 para 2.1.
7 CoP, vol 2, chapter 2, para 44, p. 33.
8 CoP, vol 2, chapter 7, para 40, p. 194; National Standards No 2, para 2.3.
9 CoP, vol 2, chapter 7, para 57, p. 198; National MHO Standards No. 2, para 2.11.
10 National Standards No.2, para 2.7.
11 CoP, vol 2,chapter 7, para 51, p 197.
12 emergency certificate: section 36(7); CoP, vol 2, chapter 7, para 63, p. 200; short-term certificate: section 44(5)(a); CoP, vol.2, chapter 2, para 58, p. 37.
13 CoP, vol 2, chapter 7, para 37, p. 193.
14 CoP, op cit, chapter 7, para 43, 195.
15 CoP, vol 2, chapter 7, para 44, p. 195.
16 section 36(12).
17 section 36(8)(a).
18 section 36(8)(b).
19 section 36(3)(b) p.22 uses the word 'likely'.
20 ref: Co P, vol 2, chapter 7, paras 80-82; p. 205.
21 CoP, vol 2, chapter 7, para 45, p 195.
22 National Standards No.2, para 2.4.
23 CoP, vol 2, chapter 7, para 45, p. 195.
24 The Code state "Such a report will be particularly important in any case where an MHO has withheld consent to the granting of the emergency detention but the certificate was granted all the same" [CoP, vol.2, chapter 7, para 45 p. 195].
25 CoP, vol 2,chapter 7, para 45, p. 195; National Standards No.2, para 2.4.
26 section 38(2).
27 section 39(a).
28 section 39(b).
29 section 38(2).
30 section 44(1) Form DET 2.
31 section 44(4)(b).
32 section 44(4)(c).
33 section 44(4)(d).
34 section 44(4)(e).
35 section 44(3)(b).
36 CoP, vol. 2, chapter 7, para 39, p. 193.
37 Form DET 2, p. 7.
38 CoP, vol 2, chapter 2, para 38, p. 31.
39 CoP, vol 2, chapter 2, para 45, p. 33.
40 CoP, vol 2, chapter 2, para 45, p. 33.
41 section 44(1).
42 CoP, vol 2, chapter 2, para 45, p 33 x-ref with chapter 7, para 45, p. 195, although only where the MHO refuses consent.
43 National Standards No. 2, para 2.4.
44 National Standards No. 2, para 2.7.
45 section 45(1)(a).
46 section 45(1)(d).
47 CoP, vol 2; chapter 2, para 60, p. 38.

Endnotes

(A) Section 45(2) Note: The reviewed Form DET 2 under "Consultation – MHO" in text box 6, allows the MHO space to record their section 45 duties. Furthermore it states "by completing this there is no longer a requirement to complete Form DET 3", that is, being unable to interview the patent or identify the patient's named person before giving consent.

(B) The CoP , vol 2, chapter 7, paras 27-29; page 190, details situations where this section of the AWI 2003 Act can be also be used to bring a patient to hospital and treat them for both a physical illness and for a mental illness. The useful practice guideline is if the patient "objects and/or requires to be detained to administer that treatment, medical staff should have recourse to procedures under the 2003 Act rather than the 2000 Act".

(C) This changed after the review of forms in 2007. All forms requiring MHO consent/consultation will now be signed by the MHO. The exception is the section 36 emergency detention certificates. The author influenced this change.

Chapter 3

Compulsory Treatment Orders

1) Introduction

- This is a substantial piece of work led by an MHO designated under section 229(1)(a). It involves multiple duties that are then presented in a composite-style application form to the Tribunal headquarters in Hamilton, South Lanarkshire, Scotland. The application form is available online and can be saved with appropriate Adobe software.[1]
- The MHO is responsible for the application. The MHO has to provide evidence at the tribunal hearing in the application and from witnesses to support the application. The RMO and other parties involved in the proposed care plan are usually the MHO's witnesses.
- The MHO has complete discretion on the choice of witness and should not see themselves as acting on behalf of the RMO.
- The Tribunal Rules of Procedure provide for a range of circumstances that arise at hearing, for example, appointing curators where the patient is mentally incapable of instructing a solicitor; if the patient or named person does not want to attend; corrections in the application; submitting late documents.
- The Tribunal can grant eight measures in any CTO as follows:

i) to be detained in a hospital;
ii) to have treatment in a hospital or in the community;
iii) to require a patient to attend a place for medical treatment;
iv) to require the patient to attend for community care services;
v) to require the patient to reside at a specified place;
vi) to allow the MHO and/or medical professional to visit;
vii) to require the patient to obtain the approval from the MHO of any proposed change of address;
viii) to require the patient to inform the MHO when moving to another address.

- The Tribunal has powers to grant a selection of these measures depending on the evidence in the application. The Tribunal cannot grant hospital/community measures simultaneously.
- Before granting the measures, the MHO as applicant has to submit paper and oral evidence from witnesses to a tribunal hearing to support the five legal tests as follows:

> i) the patient has a mental disorder;
> ii) medical treatment is available which would be likely to prevent the disorder worsening, or would be likely to alleviate the symptoms or effects of the disorder;
> iii) there would be a significant risk to the patient or to any other person if the patient was not provided with such treatment;
> iv) the patient's ability to make decisions about the provision of medical treatment is significantly impaired because of their mental disorder;
> v) the making of the compulsory treatment order is necessary.

- The Act allows the tribunal hearing to make a decision to grant a CTO on the basis of their "satisfaction", which accounts for the variety of decisions made.[2]
- This chapter will focus on the duties the MHO has to carry out to bring the evidence to a tribunal hearing. The MHO parts of Form CTO 1 have 26 text boxes. There are suggested outlines for each box by way of a template and also suggested standard template letters to use to fulfil legal duties.
- Finally, the MHO has to present the application to a tribunal hearing. In some local authorities, the MHO may not have legal representation or assistance. This chapter has guidance for the MHO in this situation.[(A)]

2) Application of CAN model to a CTO application

◆ STAGE 1: Consultation

Who is asking the MHO? What are they looking for?

Information points:

- The trigger referral to an MHO to apply for a CTO will come from different sources depending on the location and legal status of the person subject to the report. The Act uses the word "patient" for a person detained. This term will be adopted throughout the chapter.
- If a patient is already detained in hospital under an emergency detention certificate (EDC) they will be allocated a Psychiatrist – termed their responsible medical officer [RMO] – to oversee their care and treatment.[3]
- If the person is either in hospital on a voluntary basis or even living at home the approach to the MHO may be from either the patient's General Practitioner (GP) or more likely an approved medical practitioner [AMP]
- In either case, there has to be two medical assessments prepared within five days of each other. The MHO then has a further 14 days to complete the composite Form CTO 1.
- The compulsory treatment order pack includes contact details (Part 1); the MHO report (Part 2); the proposed care plan (Part 3); the CTO application itself (Part 4); and the Tribunal decision on that application (Part 5).[4] Details are as follows:

Part 1

Details of MHO, detention status and contact details of relevant parties, that is, named person, RMO, primary carer, guardian, welfare attorney, other parties relevant to this application, for example, GP, independent advocate. Record of notifications that the application is to be made under section 60 of the Act, that is, the MHO has formally written to the patient/named person, Mental Welfare Commission. This has to be done as soon as the request has been made.

Part 2

The MHO report under section 61 of the Act. This includes details of interviewing the patient and informing them of their rights, including advocacy. Other sections are details of the patient's personal circumstances/views of the mental health reports, details of advance statement, other relevant information.[5]

Part 3

Application for a compulsory treatment order:

i) **Part 3a**
Introduction – record of consultations/form of illness.[6]

ii) **Part 3a(1)(a) & (b)**
Patient's needs – details of medical treatment[7], community care or child care assessments; child assessment[8]; adult assessment[9].
Note: The MHO has a legal right to request these assessments from the local authority.[10]

Part 3a(2) (a) & (b)
Interventions required to meet the patient's needs.
Note: The MHO has to record in separate text boxes which kind of medical treatment and community services are to be provided to the patient on a compulsory or voluntary basis.[11]

iii) **Part 3a(3)(a) & (b)**
Who will carry out the interventions required to meet those needs? The MHO has to list the names and addresses of the medical and community-based professionals and where the treatment will take place for medical treatment;[12] for community-based treatment.[13]

iv) **Part 3b**
Evidence to back up proposals.
This includes sections on complying with the principles, details of alternatives and why they were not workable or practicable,

contingency plans if original proposals do not work, advance statement, that is, is this accurately reflected in the proposed care plan?, who was consulted in making this plan, risk assessment?[14]

Part 4

Application for a compulsory treatment order:

i) **Proposed Compulsory Measures**
The MHO has to outline which of the compulsory measures is being sought.[15] The measures open to the Tribunal are listed under section 66(1) in the Act. They include hospitalisation, treatment in hospital or in the community; requirement to attend on specific dates community care services, relevant services or any treatment care or service; requirement to reside at a specified place; requirement to allow access of MHO/RMO and other professionals involved with the delivery of the service; requirement to obtain approval of the MHO to any proposed change of address; requirement to inform the MHO of any change of address.

ii) **Confirmation of Application**
The MHO must confirm in writing that they carried out the legal requirements under section 63(2)(a)(ii) in Part 4; completed the relevant documents, that is, the proposed care plan, MHO report; has submitted the two Mental Health Reports and also completed the section relating to the patient's ethnicity.

Part 5

Records the tribunal hearing decisions.

Other information points

- A CTO application automatically extends a short-term detention by five working days but only when a patient is already detained under a short-term detention certificate or an extension certificate.[16]
- This further five working days in either a short-term detention

certificate (28 days), or an extension certificate (three working days) allows for medical treatment to continue under Part 16 of the Act.
- A tribunal hearing must consider the application before the additional five working days expire.

◆ STAGE 2: Assessment

Information points:

i) Mental Health Reports have to agree with diagnosis/measures sought[17]

- Two mental health reports must agree with each other on the following two issues:
    a) The two reports agree on at least one form of mental disorder from the three categories of mental illness; personality disorder; and learning disability.
    b) There has also to be agreement on the compulsory measures that should be authorised by the CTO.
- The reports have to be completed within five days of each other and properly dated.[18]
- If these conditions are not met then the CTO application is invalid. The solution would be for the MHO to have them corrected before the hearing date is fixed. The MHO can also use Tribunal Rule 21(2)[19] at the hearing that allows the Convener to accept any corrections in either the application or other submitted paper evidence.[20] This applies for evidence from any party.

ii) MHO to identify the named person [section 59]

Notes: These processes may have been done by the MHO if the patient was already detained on a short-term detention certificate. See Chapter 7 for further guidance on named person.

- The MHO must take all practicable steps to identify the name and address of the patient's named person.
- The MHO should check with the nominated named person

whether they are aware of this nomination and if they are willing to take on that role. If not they have to formally decline by writing to the local authority.[21]

- If the patient has not formally nominated a named person then the default named person would be firstly the primary carer and then the nearest relative. If the patient agrees to the primary carer or nearest relative being the default named person, they need not make a formal nomination.
- If the MHO considers the nominated named person or default named person, to be inappropriate they have a mandatory duty to apply to the initial CTO hearing of the Tribunal who can then decide whether to revoke and/or replace that named person.[22]
- The Code of Practice states "*The MHO should intervene using the powers given at section 255 only where there are clear and significant reasons for doing so.*" This could include abusive parents where the patient is under 16 years of age or even any abusive cases. Other reasons for being inappropriate could be conflicting with the patient's wishes and feelings. This is essentially a judgement for the MHO to make.[23]
- The Code of Practice advises a default or a nominated named person should always be assessed by the MHO in consultation with other professionals.[24]
- If the patient has no named person or default named person, the MHO has discretionary powers to apply to the Tribunal for a named person. This would depend on the patient's social circumstances, for example, family may be deceased or all live abroad, patient could be a long-term patient in State Hospital with no visitors.[25]
- The Code of Practice also advises where default named persons are used that "*the MHO should be careful to respect the patient's rights with respect to confidentiality and to only disclose a minimum level of information about the patient's detention*". The patient may after all wish a relative with whom they have a poor relationship to know little about their detention.[26]
- The MHO should also explain the process whereby the patient can make a declaration under section 253 of the Act or an application under section 256 of the Act to prevent a particular individual being their named person.

iii) MHO must notify certain parties of the application [section 60]

- The MHO must notify the following parties before the application is lodged:[27]
  - a) the patient;
  - b) the patient's named person; and
  - c) the Mental Welfare Commission.
- The date of this written notification should be recorded on Part 1.
- The MHO can overrule an AMP's recommendation that a patient should not be informed of the application. This should be discussed between the AMP and the MHO. The Code of Practice suggests this decision should be recorded in writing.[28]
- The MHO must also inform the person of their rights in relation to opposing the application, legal representation and of independent advocacy services. The Code of Practice states that the MHO has to avoid a "tick-box exercise" but instead be proactive in ensuring this service is made available.[29]
- The patient can oppose the application or choose to be represented by a solicitor to question aspects of the application. They can also chose any person to assist them with the application[30]. The tribunal hearing have a right to refuse this assistance if their conduct is, or is likely to be, disruptive[31].
- The patient can appeal a Tribunal's decision to make or refuse a CTO within 21 days of the hearing. This appeal process also applies to a range of other parties, including the MHO, RMO and named person.[32]
- The Code of Practice lists seven 'best practice' points which an MHO should comply with when carrying out these duties which centre around explaining the Tribunal system; putting patient in touch with a solicitor; named persons information and if necessary helping them nominate a named person, issuing leaflets on the process and contacting an independent advocate.[33]
- The Code of Practice helpfully suggests some of these tasks can be delegated to other professionals. The key person would be the patient's named nurse who, for example, can contact the solicitor.[34]

Practice points: Part 1-4

- The Form CTO 1 is composed of four parts as described above. Each part has free text boxes. They are referenced from Part 2 onwards. The MHO has to complete Parts 1-4 which have 26 free text boxes.
- The information required is specific and can be cross-referenced with other documents, principally the two mental health reports and where relevant, the social circumstances report, for example, Part 2, text box 3, p. 6 under "Details of Personal Circumstances of the Patient".
- It must be remembered this form will be read by a variety of people – patient; named person; legal representatives; Tribunal panel; medical practitioner; appeal court system. The form is therefore designed to focus on specific evidence that can later be elaborated by the MHO's witnesses as the legal process unfolds.[(B)]
- Bearing in mind the range of readers described above and the legal purpose of a Tribunal, the MHO should keep to the facts supported by evidence. Lists of services or witness opinions alone are poor evidence.
- To ease this process and avoid unnecessary verbiage, a standard template for each text box is included below for guidance. This also includes information that is of administrative value to the Tribunal staff.
- The guidance at the beginning of the Form CTO 1 reads as follows:

> *Where a text box has a reference number to the left, you can extend your response on plain paper where there is insufficient space in the box. Extension sheet(s) should be clearly labelled with the Patient's name and CHI number, and each extended response should be labelled with the appropriate text box reference number and attached to the end of the application.*

PART 1: key features/explanations (1) to (5)

Details of MHO, detention status and contact details of relevant parties:

1 CHI Number [page 1]

This stands for Community Health Index number and is a unique ten-digit number given to every person registered with the National Health Service. This applies only to patients registered in Scotland. The first six numbers relate to the patient's date of birth, for example, 8 June 1963 would read as 080663. The last four digits are the unique CHI number, for example, 080663**1200**.[35]

2 Patient's home/current address [page 1]

The revised form differentiates between the patient's home and current address. This recognises the location could depend on the patient's legal status. There is a helpful list of possible locations in the form, that is, living at home, anywhere in the community, or already detained in hospital under the Act. This prevents confusion for the Tribunal administrative staff that uses this information to send out notifications.

3 Patient's current status/MHO/RMO details [page 2]

This is self-evident although the identity of the RMO may differ for Health Trusts, that is, the community-based Psychiatrist may be the patient's RMO as opposed to the ward hospital-based Psychiatrist. The revised form now has e-mail/telephone entries that may not be appropriate to include given the range of readership described above.

4a Named person:

- The revised form now lists the three types of named persons available from the Act, that is, nominated by the patient; appointed by the Tribunal; default (primary carer or next of kin].
- The Code of Practice advises that the MHO has a role in discussing the role of a named person with any person nominated and also assessing their appropriateness for this role so there is no

point in recording a named person until this has been done (see guidance above).

- If the MHO is not sure (a) whether the nominated or default named person accepts the role; or (b) whether the MHO has had time to assess the suitability of the named person, they may wish to type "see text box 7, page 8 for details"
- The MHO could also use Tribunal Rule 45(2) and 63(4) to submit further information. This should preferably be submitted seven days before the first hearing but the Convener has discretion whether to accept submissions from any party on the hearing day itself.

4b Relevant parties including primary care/welfare attorney and guardian under the Adults with Incapacity (Scotland) 2000 Act, page 3:

- The Act cross-references the AWI 2000 Act by requesting whether or not the patient has a welfare guardian or a welfare attorney. They have a right to be notified of a tribunal hearing. These terms are explained in a Note beside the boxes.[36]
- This right also applies to a primary carer if different to the patient's named person, that is, someone who provides a substantial amount of care on a regular basis. The primary carer, for example, could be receiving a carer's allowance benefit. This excludes, however, a contracted or volunteer carer.

Notes to 4a & b above:

i) Named person - declaration by person.[(C)]

The Tribunal is not bound by a declaration made by a person under section 253(1) stating they do not wish either the nominated or a default named person to act as their named person. The MHO may not have an alternative choice of named person for the detained patient, or may disagree with this declaration.

Oddly, however, a detained patient of any age can apply to the Tribunal under section 256(1)(a) to have a named person removed on the grounds that they are inappropriate. Where the patient is a child, this could include their parent or a primary carer, for example, grandparent/sibling over aged 16 years, but not the local authority.

Note: see Chapter 7 for further guidance on named person.

ii) Identity of welfare attorney/guardian

The MHO should check the particular powers in either a welfare guardianship or a welfare power of attorney for consent to medical treatment powers.[37]

Legal reference:

a) welfare guardian – AWI(S) Act 2000, section 58(1); 2003 Act, section 64(3)(c),.

b) welfare attorney – AWI(S) 2000 Act section 16(5); 2003 Act, section 64(3)(d)

5 **Record of contact details of other Relevant Parties**

- This may include relevant persons whom the Tribunal have notified under sections 64(2) and 64(3) as discussed above. The RMO should be the standard witness. The MHO may want to include the second medical opinion from the AMP/GP if there is anything in the report that differs or augments the RMO's report. The medical reports may be unclear, hence the MHO's right to consider requesting their presence.[(D)]
- The patient's legal representative and the Tribunal can cite their own witnesses but would have to pay their fees. The MHO cannot cite witnesses in the same way. Payment for a GP to attend would come from their health authority, unless the Tribunal cited them, in which case the Tribunal would meet the relevant expenses.[(E)]
- Relevant parties as witnesses could be the community/ward-based nursing staff who know the patient well or a community care service provider where a community-based CTO is sought. The MHO may want to include the named nurse or any such relevant party as a witness.
- It may be that the RMO is not actually treating the patient in the ward but instead has delegated another AMP to treat the patient. This RMO, delegated under section 230(3), may not be the second medical opinion.
- The Tribunal will send notification letters to all of the relevant persons listed. It is important, therefore, to have their full name/address/ telephone number for the Tribunal staff to contact them if the hearing date is fixed at short notice.[38]

Legal references:

Tribunal Rules – Scottish Statutory Instrument 2005 No. 519 [the legal name for Regulations]; The Mental Health Tribunal for Scotland (Practice and Procedure) (No. 2) Rules 2005.

Website: type "Scottish legislation" under search.

Part 1: Record of notifications about the CTO application.

Note: see Stage 3, Part 1 below for details of the three letters.

PART 2: MHO report under section 61 (text boxes 1 to 7)

MHO to confirm that they have interviewed the patient; informed them about the application and of availability of independent advocacy services; taken appropriate steps to ensure the patient has access to this service.

Text box 1

This allows the MHO to detail why they could not interview the patient.

Text box 2

Detailed steps MHO has taken to comply with section 61(2).

Suggested standard template text:

i) Informed patient about i) process of application; ii) the right to oppose the application – verbally and in writing on [insert date]. Patient accepted/refused to take the letter but understood the procedure. [ref: using standard Letter 1 in Chapter 9 witnessed by Staff Nurse X.]

ii) Wrote to X Advocacy Services asking them to make contact with patient. [ref: using standard letter 4 in Appendix 1].

iii) Spoke to patient's named nurse/ward staff for an update on treatment.

iv) Current position: [insert date] – patient opposing the application.
He/she does/does not want legal representation/unable to instruct a solicitor.

Text box 3

MHO report under section 61(4)
Details of Personal Circumstances of the Patient.

Suggested standard text: guidance.

> The MHO may wish to select headings already available from the statutory social circumstances report. These headings are quoted directly from the regulations Scottish Statutory Instrument 2005 No. 310. There are 19 headings in regulations lettered (a) to (s). The Form CTO 1 in text box 3, page 6 allows the MHO discretion in disclosing details about the patient's personal circumstances using the term "*in so far as relevant for the purposes of the application*"[39]

Note: see Chapter 8 for guidance on social circumstances report.

- The MHO may wish to include the headings within the text box itself. This would save duplication of effort.
- Another approach could be to summarise key features in the patient's life that have led to this application as follows:[40]

a. Background information – brief family history.
b. Adult years.
c. Current life-style.
d. Events leading to this application – for example, section 44 certificate.
e. Risks at point of admission.
f. Update – relevant issues.

Text box 4 & 5

MHO's view on the mental health reports.
The MHO may wish to list the sections referred to in the question and then report their views accordingly.

Suggested standard text: (example supplied)

> Views on content with respect to:
> i) Section 57(4)(a) – mental disorder.
> In agreement. Formal diagnosis made on (insert date)
> ii) Section 57(4)(b) – available to the patient.
> In agreement.
> Patient beginning to slowly respond to medication.
> iii) Section 57(4)(e) – CTO is necessary.
> Voluntary measures would not work as patient likely to affect his/her own discharge.

Note: The Form CTO 1 allows the MHO to offer a view(s) of the above 3 aspects of treatment "*as well as all other significant aspects of the reports*". The range of views can be four-fold – agree; agree with reservations; disagree or adopt a neutral position[41]

Other significant aspects of the report:

> Discussion with Dr. X, RMO on (insert date)
>
> *The main reason for this application is to ensure patient continues with his medication. Patient is accepting nursing care. Patient lacks insight into his illness so would not accept either hospital treatment or community-based treatment voluntarily. Patient currently very angry at being detained. Dr.X. has assessed patient as capable of instructing a solicitor, although patient has chosen to speak to the Tribunal without representation. [example material]*

The MHO can repeat this template in text box 5, that is, the second mental health report.

Additional Guidance Notes:

a) The Code of Practice states the MHO has a right to express an independent view on the mental health reports. If there is dissent then the issues in conflict should be presented to the Tribunal to make a judgement on whether or not to grant an application.[42]

b) Similarly if the MHO disagrees with any proposed community-based measures in the mental health reports, the Code of Practice suggests the MHO has some veto in the matter as follows:

> *"Where the practitioners have recommended community-based compulsory measures in the mental health reports, it would be good practice for the MHO to consider the extent to which the issues described at paragraphs 29 to 33 above have been taken into account before including these compulsory measures in the final CTO application."* [43]

c) The Act recognises it may be impracticable for the MHO to consult the relevant persons. The MHO should therefore state this here quoting section 62(7) of the Act.

d) The MHO may feel uncomfortable using the term "patient" throughout the evidence. This is a legal term and therefore the correct legal address even though the subject of the report may not be an inpatient.

Text box 6

Advance Statement [section 275]

The MHO should leave this blank if the patient has not made an Advance Statement. The option of recording the patient's past and present wishes are included in Part 3b, text box 18, titled: "evidence to back up proposals", that is, application of principles. This is non-statutory evidence but optional if the MHO is able to elicit the patient's wishes (see under Part 3b below).

Text box 7

Other Information

- This allows the MHO an opportunity to raise issues not stated in other parts of the form. This could be named persons, that is, whether or not one has been nominated/default; their suitability; whether the named person agrees to take on this role.
- The MHO could use this text box to inform the Tribunal whether the patient wishes to be legally represented. If the patient cannot instruct a solicitor the MHO may wish to ask the Tribunal for a "Person of Skill" assessment under Rule 155(3) of the Tribunal Rules. This appointment is discretionary.[F]

PART 3: Proposed Care Plan [text boxes 8 to 23]

This is divided into five subsections, which are obscurely numbered

Part 3a

Introduction [text box 8-9].

Part 3a(1)

Patient's needs – medical/community care.

i) 3a(1)(a): Patient's medical needs [text box 10];
ii) 3a(1)(b): Patient's community services needs [text box 11];

Part 3a(2)

Interventions Required to Meet the Patient's Needs medical/ community care.

i) 3a(2)(a): Patient's medical needs.
Compulsory and Voluntary basis [text box 12 & 13];
ii) 3a(2)(b): Patient's community services needs.
Compulsory and Voluntary basis [text box 14 & 15].

Part 3a(3)

Who will carry out the interventions required to meet those needs?

i) 3a(3)(a): List of who is to provide medical treatment [text box 16];

ii) 3a(3)(b): List of who is to provide community care services [text box 17].

Part 3b

Evidence to back up proposals [text boxes 18-23]

i) Text box 18 Application of the Principles under section 1-3 of the 2003 Act.

ii) Text box 19 Alternatives tried to avoid compulsory powers and why they were deemed not to be workable or practicable.

iii) Text box 20 Contingency plans.

iv) Text box 21 Wishes in advance statements [compared to text box 6]

v) Text box 22 Who was consulted in drawing up the proposed care plan?

vi) Text box 23 Issues of risk and how they were taken into account.

List of suggested templates for text box 10 to 23.

This example is based on a patient who requires a hospital based CTO with treatment. The wording can be varied for community-based measures while still using the same statutory references required in the application form. The texts are brief to allow for individual MHO writing styles. The MHO should, however, remember the range of readers, that is, professional people, patient and patient's named person.

Text box 10

Patient's medical needs

Section 329(i) (a) to (e) – range of medical treatment.

i) section 329(i)(a) – nursing.
Applicable as patient would not take medication voluntarily.

ii) section 329(i)(b) – care.
Not applicable as patient can care for self.

iii) section 329(i)(c) – psychological intervention.
Not applicable at this stage in medical treatment.

iv) section 329(i)(d) – habilitation (including education, and training in work, social and independent living skills).
Not applicable at this stage in medical treatment.

v) section 329(i)(e) -- rehabilitation (re-learning skills already acquired as listed in iv) above.
Not applicable at this stage in medical treatment.

Text box 11

Patient's community services needs

- Not applicable. A social work referral would be made if this were necessary after patient regains the capacity to choose whether or not he/she requires a community care assessment. Given patient's good self-care skills when well, it is unlikely he/she would require or see a need for a needs-led assessment.
- This would be in accord with the principle in section 3(a) – patient's present and past wishes and feelings; and section 4 – minimum restriction. A suspension certificate under section 127 of the 2003 Act would presumably raise the need for community care services, if any.

Text box 12

Compulsory medical treatment
Section 329(i) – range of medical treatment.

i) section 329(i)(a) – nursing: assessment; containment; giving of medication.
ii) section 329(i)(b) – care.
Not applicable as patient is accepting care.
iii) section 329(i)(c) – psychological intervention.
Not applicable at this stage in medical treatment.
iv) section 329(i)(d) – habilitation (including education, and training in work, social and independent living skills)
v) section 329(i)(e) – rehabilitation (re-learning skills already acquired as listed in iv) above.
Not applicable at this stage in medical treatment.

Text box 13

Voluntary medical treatment
Section 329(i) – range of medical treatment. From RMO's comment, the patient is not able to agree voluntarily to any forms of medical treatment at this stage owing to the paranoid nature of his/her illness.

i) section 329(i)(a) – nursing.
ii) section 329(i)(b) – care.
Patient needs regular nourishment; to be in a safe, risk-free environment.
iii) section 329(i)(c) – psychological intervention.
iv) section 329(i)(d) – habililitation (including education, and training in work, social and independent living skills).
v) section 329(i)(e) – rehabilitation (re-learning skills already acquired as listed in iv) above.

Text box 14

Community care services on a compulsory basis

- Not applicable as the measures proposed are hospital-based only.
- The RMO and the MHO have statutory duties of assessment, monitoring, supervision; reviewing and support to the patient which would continue should a suspension certificate be issued under section 127 of the Act.

Text box 15

Community care services on a voluntary basis.

Note: It is not possible to write voluntary care plan proposals, as the patient is unable to agree at this stage in his illness.

Dr. X, RMO, states the voluntary aspect of a care plan could be that his community psychiatric nurse sees the patient regularly at least fortnightly when in the community. Dr X also states that the patient would be seen regularly (at least 3-monthly) as an outpatient.

This would be subject to patient's agreement, which has not been an issue in the past.

Text box 16

List of who is to provide medical treatment.

Dr. X, RMO, appointed under section 230(1) of the 2003 Act, or any other RMO delegated by the hospital managers under section 230(3) of the 2003 Act. This delegated function is currently carried out by Dr. X, RMO/Consultant Psychiatrist responsible for Ward Y., IPCU, Z. Hospital. Dr. X would be responsible for patient's care when he/she is transferred to the open ward and eventually discharged.

Any mental health nurse employed by W. NHS Board.
Hospital address for treatment: Z.

Text box 17

List of who is to provide community care services
Not applicable to the measures sought. Or listed as appropriate.

Note: This need only be the named Manager of a Care Provider/ Chief Social Work Officer. It is not necessary to specify the names of specific professionals.

Text box 18

Application of the Principles under section 1-3 of the 2003 Act.
Principles section 1-3 (sample material)

1) Section 1(3)(a) – patient's present and past wishes and feelings relevant to the discharge of the function. Patient is currently angry at being detained. Past wishes: patient would not want to be hospitalised. (source: Y, CPN)
2) Section 1(3)(b) – views of patient's named person/carer/ guardian/welfare attorney. My home visit to patient's father on [insert date] indicates he supports the application.
3) Section 1(3)(c) – patient participation. Patient states he has no interest in the CTO application proceedings. He also left my interview as he said he was beginning to lose his temper. Staff Nurse X was present at this interview. [insert date].
4) Section 1(3)(d) – provision of information. I tried to discuss this with him on the same interview and also give him a summary letter but he refused to look at it.
5) Section 1(3)(e) – range of options. Given the history of a build up to the patient's illness over a long period and the fact this has gone untreated suggests this admission helped to bring the result of patient's illness to a head. The use of civil compulsory powers therefore became the most appropriate option.

6) Section 1(3)(f) – maximum benefit. The same argument in section 1(3)(e) applies.
7) Section 1(3)(h) – non-discrimination. Patient given the same dignified care as for other patients in the ward.
8) Section 1(4) – minimum restriction. Patient does not believe he is ill and wants to leave the ward. He understands he is detained on a short-term detention certificate until [insert date]. Patient angry at being detained and wants to oppose this application.
9) Section 6 – provision of appropriate services. ("Reciprocity"[44]). Given patient remains unwell, hospital-based treatment remains the most appropriate option at this stage. Hopefully the provision of continuing care will change to community-based medical treatment involving a community psychiatric nurse monitoring treatment. This may be done initially using a suspension certificate under section 127(1) and later on a voluntary basis when patient makes a fuller recovery.
10) Section 3 – equal opportunities. This is standard hospital policy towards all patients.

Note: If the patient is under 18 years of age, the MHO should describe in what way the application of the ten principles above secured the fundamental principle of welfare for that patient.[45]

Text box 19

Alternatives tried to avoid compulsory powers and why they were deemed not to be workable or practicable

The main reasons for hospital-based detention and medical treatment are documented in both Mental Health Reports:

i) Patient went missing from his home for 3 days. Alternative of a voluntary admission not feasible as patient presenting as threatening and did not want to remain in the open ward.
ii) Evidence of self-neglect.
iii) Patient still displays no insight into his illness, therefore would not be able to agree voluntarily to medical treatment.

This is evidence that patient continues to require compulsory medical treatment to alleviate or improve his symptoms.
Note: see section 64(5) for detailed wording

Text box 20

Contingency plans

- Given this is a proposed hospital-based measure; there are no contingency plans. If the hospital detention with treatment measures were not granted, it is unlikely patient would remain informally or accept any community-based services.
- The named nurse has known patient from a previous admission and told me the patient normally takes about six weeks to stabilise his medication.

Text box 21

Wishes of advance statements [compared to text box 6]

Patient has not made an advance statement. Patient's wishes are clearly that he does not want to be in hospital. I checked this with X, CPN, who confirmed patient would not wish to have a hospital admission in any circumstances.

Text box 22

Who was consulted in drawing up the proposed care plan

1) Dr. X, RMO;
2) Dr. Y, AMP – to discuss their Mental Health Reports;
3) Staff Nurse Z., named nurse – to discuss on-going patient management;
4) P. – community psychiatric nurse [CPN].
   Staff Nurse Z states the nursing/care tasks would be as follows:

i) ensure patient takes medication and to maintain this until compulsory powers are not required and patient agrees to do this voluntarily,
ii) provide direction for daily living skills.
iii) provide emotional support to patient who at times can be distressed due to paranoid thinking.

The applicant hopes to have Staff Nurse Z at the tribunal hearing to update her work with the patient.

Text box 23

Issues of risk and how they were taken into account

Staff Nurse Z. offered the following risk issues.

Due to deterioration in patient's mental state he has neglected himself. He was also verbally aggressive and threatening towards other patients and staff on admission. He would not voluntarily take his medication. He has still to reach the therapeutic level in his medication, which can take up to six weeks. This means patient and other people would remain at risk if the hospital detention/hospital-based medical treatment were not granted.

Evidence for this

(1) Discussion with Staff Nurse Z, named nurse (see paragraph above).
(2) Medical notes at point of admission that describes patient's unkempt state; his verbal/physical aggression and also lack of insight into his illness.
    On-going notes also describe patient's unwillingness to think about the CTO application. Patient believes he will be discharged when the section 44 expires.
(3) Discussion with P., CPN, who has known patient since [insert].
(4) Reference to the two mental health reports on page 7.

PART 4: Application for a compulsory treatment order

The MHO has to shade from the eight measures available. For the measures not sought, the MHO could insert a standard sentence as follows:

"No evidence submitted to support this measure."

This might then avoid the possibility of the tribunal hearing trying to seek "evidence" of their own to grant other measures not proposed. The Tribunal could grant an interim CTO for the applicant to obtain such evidence.

◆ STAGE 3: Notifications by MHO

- There are several notification duties an MHO has to fulfil in the process of completing the Form CTO 1. These have been identified as Letters 1-4 in Part 1 above.
- There are however additional letters included here which may ease the legal progress of an application.

Statutory notification letters:

PART 1

Record of notifications about the CTO application

Suggestion: The MHO may want to use standard letters for these notifications. They are listed as follows. They are in Chapter 9 and numbered according to chapter.

Letter 1: [section 61(1)(a)]
MHO to patient informing of rights/availability of advocacy services/informing patient the application is being made.

Letter 2: [section 60(1)(b)]
MHO to named person informing him/her of the CTO application.

Letter 3: [section 60(1)(c)]
MHO to Mental Welfare Commission about the CTO application.

PART 2

MHO report under section 61 of the 2003 Act

Letter 4: [section 60(2)(c)(ii)]
MHO to independent advocacy services about the CTO application.

Suggested additional letter (named persons):

Letter 1: MHO to named person confirming their agreement to be either a nominated/default named person.
Letter 2: Named person to MHO declining the nomination.
Letter 3: MHO to patient's RMO confirming the patient's named person.
Letter 4: MHO to Tribunal/Commission re: steps taken to establish a named person and also reasons why MHO did not nominate an alternative named person. [section 255(5)].
Letter 5: MHO to Tribunal re: inappropriateness of an apparent named person [section 255(6)].
Letter 6: Named person [nominated or default] writes to the Tribunal requesting no notification and also to waive their consultation rights for changes in the proposed measures or granting an interim CTO.

Legal references for Tribunal notifications:

i) Section 255(3)
MHO establishes whether the patient has a named person
ii) Section 64(3)(b)
Tribunal notifies named person.
iii) Section 255(6)(b)
MHO deems named person (whether nominated or default) to be inappropriate
iv) Section 257(2)

Tribunal can grant an order disposing of the named person if the MHO deems them inappropriate and applies to the Tribunal on this basis. The Tribunal has discretion under section 257(2)(b) to have another named person appointed but there may be none available in some cases.

v) Section 64(3)(c) &(d)
Tribunal notifies welfare guardian/attorney.

vi) Section 64(3)(h) p. 42
Tribunal notifies the primary carer.

Note: see Chapter 7 for details on named person and letter order.

◆ Administration issues

1. The Form CTO 1 plus two medical reports have to be lodged with the Tribunal headquarters in Hamilton before the 14th day of the last medical examination, which counts as one of the fourteen days.[46]
2. The Tribunal has no time limits to arrange a hearing if the patient is not already under a civil compulsory power. This would probably apply where someone is still in the community and the MHO is seeking community-based compulsory powers.
3. If the patient is already subject to a short-term/extension certificate, the Tribunal has the option to exercise the right to extend the existing certificate by five working days to allow time to set a hearing date.[47]
4. The best means of posting the CTO application would be by Special Delivery, which guarantees next-day delivery.
5. The caseworker in Hamilton – legally known as the Clerk in the Tribunal Rules – will contact the MHO and RMO by telephone in advance of the hearing. This is useful so the MHO can organise the witnesses.
6. The caseworker has to send the patient and the patient's named person a copy of the application and any accompanying documents mentioned in section 63(3), that is, the two medical reports and the proposed care plan.[48]
7. Any relevant person receives a standard letter from the caseworker

about the hearing date/measures proposed and that they can attend to give evidence, with or without legal representation or assistance.[49]

8. The MHO can submit additional documents for evidence any time up to and including the hearing date itself. The MHO should have sufficient copies of additional papers for the three Tribunal members, patient's legal representatives.[50]
9. The MHO can withdraw the application at any time up to and including the date of the hearing.
10. If the Tribunal has already granted an order, for example, an interim CTO under section 65(2), they will only accept written notice of revocation from the RMO, even though the RMO would have completed Form REV 2. This can be faxed.
11. At the conclusion of the hearing, the MHO will receive a copy of Part 6, signed by the Convener. Fuller details of their decision should follow within the 21-day appeal period. These are called "Full Findings and Reasons" reasons for granting or refusing the CTO, adding any recorded matters, disputing the type of mental disorder. This statement could then be used for an appeal to the sheriff principal under section 320(1)(b).

The Tribunal headquarters address is:

The Mental Health Tribunal for Scotland
First Floor, Hamilton Business Park
Caird Park, Hamilton ML3 0QA
Telephone: 01698 390000.

◆ Presentation by MHO without legal assistance – suggested format (Steps 1 to 4)

Introduction

The Tribunal Rules allow the MHO options to have legal representation, with assistance or to conduct the case alone. The Rules do not specify the professional nature of this assistance, so any assistance could be from an experienced MHO colleague and not necessarily a Council solicitor.[51]

The following are guidelines for the MHO leading the evidence alone.

Step 1

MHO summarises the reasons for the application

- In this case it might be helpful for the MHO to have already provided a summary of facts and evidence in a covering letter to the Convener. The MHO could then read out from this letter at the tribunal hearing by way of introducing the application and steadying their nerves! The MHO can also update the position verbally as each point is covered.
- Format of facts/evidence could be as follows:

Summary details in letter form and also to be read out at the hearing by way of introduction.

1. Request the Tribunal to implement Rule 21(2) to amend any documents, for example, wrong date or diagnosis or Rule 63(4) to lodge additional documents as evidence.
2. Whether or not the MHO is seeking an interim CTO under section 65(2).[(G)]
3. Patient's age, current address/statute, including start and expiry dates.
4. MHO should state whether or not patient agrees or is opposing the application. This could be the whole or part of the application.
5. Patient's status, for example, married; single, living alone or with others.
6. Named person – identity and type, that is, nominated/default. Confirm appropriateness or inappropriateness of the named person. If the latter, the MHO is then required to write to the (same) tribunal hearing why the named person is inappropriate and suggest an alternative named person [section 255(6)].
7. The MHO should state whether or not the named person agrees with the application. If the named person is absent from the hearing, the MHO should provide a statement from the named person as to whether or not they wish to waive their right to be consulted about any decisions arising from this hearing. [section 65(4)]

8. Confirm the two mental health reports agree the person has a diagnosis of mental disorder, at least one of the possible three types, and agree with the proposed measures [section 57(5)(a) & (b)].
9. Describe briefly why the patient was admitted to hospital or is to be admitted under this application. The MHO could quote the text box references from the mental health report and the application form. This will help to focus the Tribunal members on specific issues. Text boxes 2-6 in the mental health reports correspond with the five legal tests for a CTO under section 64(5) (a) to (e).
10. If the patient is already in hospital, describe improvements as a result of treatment and what treatment needs to continue on a compulsory basis, for example, medication. To assist the hearing, the MHO could quote text box 4 in the mental health report. [section 57(4)(d)].
11. State what the proposed measures are and highlight their benefit. [section 57(4)(e)].
12. Finally, include any other relevant information in the medical reports [section 57(4)(g)].

Additional points of information:

1. MHO should state whether or not they will be legally represented or act alone.
2. State whether patient is able to instruct a solicitor. The Tribunal then has discretion whether or not to appoint a "person of skill"[52] under the Tribunal Rule 55(3). It would be helpful if this were done in advance of the hearing. It may be the MHO considers they have sufficient evidence in the application for this right to be waived by the Tribunal. Now is the time for the MHO to state their case to save the need for a further hearing.
3. The difficulties that arise in taking this approach is if the patient is not present or not represented, the medical reports do not "speak for themselves". They may or may not be accepted at the hearing, as they would then be submitted as paper evidence.
4. The best position for the MHO as applicant would be to have at least the RMO present to speak of their report in order for it to be

held up to cross-examination and tested, otherwise it is quite weak. All that changes if a patient does not challenge the reports or any witnesses. This highlights the importance of having the patient or his representative at the hearing.

5. The MHO may wish to apply for an interim CTO to allow the patient time to seek legal advice if the application is being opposed. This is often done in agreement with the patient's case solicitor. The Convener of the hearing will in any case seek a common agreement. Evidence is required to be led by the MHO to support the granting of an interim CTO.[53]
6. The interim CTO may be the "normal" route to allow both parties sufficient time to prepare their case. The Tribunal can also grant an interim CTO if they want to appoint a Curator ad litem.[54]
7. It is important to note the Tribunal must first consider whether to make an interim CTO where a patient is already subject to a further five working days detention under section 68 to allow a hearing date to be fixed. The Tribunal Rules call this "a first hearing".[55]
8. If the Tribunal decide to grant an interim CTO, they can issue a list of directions available to the MHO on further evidence, including asking for specific reports.[56]
9. If the Tribunal choose not to grant an interim order, only then can they consider the MHO's application for a CTO.[57]
10. The MHO should state who their witnesses are or, if absent, submit their written evidence. The MHO can also cite Tribunal Rule 63(4) if they wish to change or update their evidence, for example, include new witnesses/reports.
11. The MHO may wish to advise the RMO to take the patient's notes to the Tribunal hearing for reference instead of just relying on the medical report

Step 2

MHO considers patient's views at the hearing

- If a patient agrees that a CTO should be granted, the Tribunal still has to be satisfied all the five legal criteria in section 64(5)(a) to (e) for compulsory detention are met. The legal test is the Tribunal's "*satisfaction*".[58]

- If the patient opposes the CTO and does so through their solicitor, it is possible that the solicitor may wish to seek an independent medical opinion on behalf of his client. In those circumstances, the MHO can suggest seeking an interim CTO from the Tribunal. This is the same test as for a full CTO except the last test of 'necessity' relates to a shorter period.[59]

Step 3

MHO questions the medical witness
Legal test: 2003 Act [section 64(5)(a) to (f)]

Preliminary questions:
- If the Tribunal Convener does not check this, a good starting place would be to confirm with them the following matters:
  a. that they are, in fact, the RMO for the patient.
  b. how long they have been involved with the patient.
- Supplementary questions may be required as new evidence emerges.

1. Mental disorder [section 64(5)(a)]
  a. whether or not they consider that the patient is suffering from a mental disorder.
  b. the nature of the disorder and the symptoms and episodes displayed.

2. Medical treatment – available [section 64(5)(b)]
  a. the medical treatment the patient is currently receiving.
  b. the medication that the patient is presently receiving (including how that medication is administered and frequency of medication).
  c. the effects of medication (and other medical treatment).
  d. the patient's current condition.
  e. any improvements in the patient's condition since admission to hospital.
  f. the RMO's anticipation of the effect of the proposed medical treatment on the patient.

3. **Significant risk to health, safety or welfare of the person or safety of any other person: section 64(5)(c)**
   a. what risks the patient poses to himself.
   b. whether the patient poses a risk to others, and if so what those risks are.

4. **Significant impairment of person's decision-making about medical treatment [section 64(5)(d)]**
   The RMO's opinion on the patient's ability to make decisions about the provision of medical treatment. This must include evidence to support that opinion.

5. **Is this order necessary? [section 64(5)(e)]**
   a. whether or not the RMO considers that the CTO is necessary.
   b. (if appropriate) the RMO's summary of why a CTO is necessary.

Step 4

MHO questions the named nurse/social worker

Note: These questions will vary according to the patient's circumstances. The named nurse may be unwilling to give an opinion whether a CTO is required. This should be respected and the questions suitably worded in agreement with the named nurse.

1. **Witness 1: Staff Nurse, ward x**
   a. What are patient's nursing needs at the moment?
   b. Have there been improvements since admission?
   c. Would patient be able to receive medical treatment voluntarily in the ward?

2. **Witness 2: Allocated social worker**
   a. How long have you known the patient?
   b. What attempts have been made to care for patient when living at home and what have been his responses?
   c. Do you support the CTO application for hospital-based treatment?

◆ MHO's views on the CTO application-guidance

- The MHO is the only person who can apply for a CTO. The Act allows the MHO to express a view on the mental health reports which may vary as follows:

  - support the application;
  - support it with reservations,
  - adopt a neutral position, for example, if they do not know enough about the particular type of psychiatry, say, of children.
  - disagree with the application.

- The MHO should, therefore, state their position at the outset of the hearing.
- There is a compulsory element in stating a view. Text boxes 4 and 5 in Form CTO 1 relates to section 57(4)(a)(b) and (e). The MHO has scope, therefore, to consider adopting different views in the light of each subsection. The guidance heading in Form CTO 1 also expects the MHO to offer a view *" on all other significant aspects of the reports."*
- The Code of Practice helpfully reminds the MHO their views are focused through the principles and also whether or not the criteria for compulsory powers are met. Furthermore, the guidance suggests the MHO would have a veto role where community-based measures are being proposed.
- It should be borne in mind a neutral position is still a view. It may be, for example, the MHO has not been given sufficient information either orally or in the medical reports to form a view. The MHO may know little or nothing about that particular aspect of Psychiatry, for example, child or old age psychiatry.
- As stated before, the key issue for the Tribunal is to hear sufficient evidence in relation to the five legal tests in section 64(5).

Note: see Appendix 2 for subsequent events after a CTO is granted.

Footnotes:

1 Mental Welfare Commission website:.mwcscot.org.uk . Follow the trail for "New Forms".
2 section 64(4)(a). The MHO may think some of the Tribunal decisions surprising and maybe even disappointing. Perhaps it is best for the MHO not to hold any expectation.
3 section 230(1).
4 The author is grateful to Les Nicholson, Project Manager, MWC for advanced sight of these forms.
5 section 61(2).
6 section 62 (4); section 62(7).
7 section 62 (5)(b).
8 section 62 (5)(c)(i).
9 section 62 (5)(c)(ii).
10 section 227.
11 Form CTO 1, text boxes 12-15. The voluntary basis list seems improbable to implement in a compulsory treatment order. The author is stumped.
12 section 62 (5)(d).
13 section 62(5)(e).
14 section 1; 2, 3; section 1(4); section 61(4)(g), section 62(3).
15 section 62(5)(g).
16 section 68 ; CoP, vol 2 chapter 3, para 77, p 85. A "working day" is defined in s.47(8) , that is, weekends plus Scottish bank holidays. See Endnote (E), chapter 1 for details on Scottish Bank holidays.
17 section 57(5)(a) & (b).
18 section 58(3). These are not 5 working days in that it can include weekends/ Scottish bank holidays. Working days only apply to detention periods. The examination days are from Day 1 to Day 5.
19 Tribunal Rules are published as a Scottish Statutory Instrument. Year 2005/No.519.
20 Inexperienced GPs may, for example, tick all the eight measures, not knowing the Tribunal can only grant hospital and community-based measures separately.
21 section 251(6) – primary carer, & section 254(5) – nearest relative; CoP, vol 2, chapter 3, para 45, p 75. See standard letter in Chapter 9 for a named person to use where they wish to decline either the nomination by the patient or a default nomination as primary carer or nearest relative.
22 section 255(6) – MHO duty; section 257(2) – Tribunal response. Note: The Code of Practice states "The MHO should intervene using the powers given at section 255 only where there are clear and significant reasons for doing so" [CoP, vol 2, chapter 3, para 42, p. 74].
23 As an aside, the MHO may wish to refer the apparent named person to their local authority vulnerable adults procedure.
24 CoP, vol. 2; chapter 3, para 42, p. 74.
25 section 255(4)(b) & (7)(b) – the word "may" is used allowing for discretion.
26 CoP, vol 2, chapter 3, para 43, p 74; National Standards No. 2, para 2.4.
27 The suggested timescale in the Act states "the MHO shall, as soon as practicable after the duty to make the application arises (and in any event, before making the application) give notice that the application is to be made" [section 60(1)].
28 section 60(2); CoP, vol 2, chapter 3, para 49, p. 75.
29 section 61(2)(b) to (d), ; CoP, vol. 2; chapter 3, para 52, p. 76.

30 Tribunal Rule 54 & 69. Rule 69 has six subsections which attempt to ensure this disruptive person has alternative means of being represented for example, if it is the patient, the appointment of a Curator ad litem under Rule 55(1).
31 Tribunal Rule 69. Rule 69 has six subsections which attempt to ensure this disruptive person has alternative means of being represented for example, if it is the patient, the appointment of a Curator ad litem under Rule 55(1).
32 section 320(1)(b); appellants are listed in section 320(5).
33 CoP, vol 2, chapter 3, para 57, p. 78 ; National Standards No. 2, para 2.1.
34 CoP, vol 2, chapter 3, para 52, p. 76.
35 The CHI number should also be used when contacting the Tribunal administration in Hamilton as their own reference numbers change according to the type of application, for example, CTOs or reviews.
36 Tribunal Rule 6(4) lists the type of information the welfare attorney/guardian would receive, that is, administration details/date of hearing/ the right to legal representation. Only the patient and named person receives a full copy of the CTO application , that is, the two medical reports/Form CTO 1 [Tribunal Rule 6(2)].
37 This information should be available from the Public Guardian's Office, Falkirk, Stirlingshire [telephone: 01324 678300], quoting section 10(1)(b) of the AWI(s) 2000 Act.
38 Tribunal Rule 56(3).
39 section 61(4)(f).
40 These headings can be varied according to the patient's personal circumstances.
41 Franks, R A, Cobb, D. (2005) Mental Health(Care and Treatment)(Scotland) Act 2003, General Note for section 61, p. 82.
42 CoP, vol 2, chapter 3, para 61- 63, p. 80.
43 CoP, vol 2, chapter 3, para 62, p. 81.
44 This is a much over-used word and can be misleading as it assumes an automatic right to services.
45 section 2(1), p. 3.
46 section 57(7).
47 section 68(1) Note: working days excludes weekends and Scottish Bank holidays. See Endnote (E), Chapter 1 for details.
48 Tribunal Rule 6(2).
49 Tribunal Rule 6(4)(e).
50 Tribunal Rule 45 & 63(4).
51 Tribunal Rule 54(1) & (3).
52 "Person of skill" is often a solicitor.
53 section 65(2).
54 Tribunal Rule 55(2).
55 Tribunal Rule 8(2). This applies where the patient is already detained under a short term or an extension certificate.
56 Rule 8(4)(a). The MHO may wish to refer to this list by way of requesting how to prepare for the next hearing. Some hearings are more proactive than others.
57 Tribunal Rule 8(2).
58 section 64(4)(a).
59 section 65(6)(b) – , that is, the necessity test.

Endnotes:

(A) The author prefers to lead his own evidence as it leads to a more informal tone at the hearing. The proviso is a well-prepared application which then allows discussion to lead from the evidence rather than just about the evidence. The Convener is charged with the responsibility of conducting the hearing, which may also include helping a straying applicant without legal assistance!

(B) The author frequently advises MHO colleagues to distinguish between "blood" information, that is, feeling, fact and opinion in an assessment as opposed to " legal" information – fact supported by evidence. This is the kind of information required by a Tribunal to test the detention criteria using section 64(5) (a) to (e). This view is emphasised by Eileen Davie, President of the Mental Health Tribunal in the Newsletter for MHOs in Scotland where she states the Tribunal role is not to "case conference"a CTO application but instead to ensure "a patient's legal rights are protected and observed at all time" [Issue 13, Autumn/Winter 2006/07]

(C) Section 250(1)(a). The legal age definition of a person is aged 16 years and over. Similarly, the named person must be over 16 years of age. The legal assumption too is the named person is ordinarily resident in the UK. This is detailed in relation to the nearest relative default nomination in section 254(6)(c). If both the service user and the nearest relative are ordinarily resident abroad then the nomination is valid. This is stated by implication under section 254(6)(c). I am grateful to Patrick, H (2006), Mental Health, Incapacity and the Law in Scotland, chapter 4, para 4.06, p 55. Totell Publishing for making this distinction

(D) If the additional witnesses are not available to attend a hearing, the MHO may want to consider requesting the Tribunal implement Tribunal Rule 71(1)(a) – "to provide a signed statement, or evidence in such form as the Tribunal thinks fit." Rule 71(2) gives a video-link as another method for an absent witness or relevant person as listed in section 64(3), to give evidence. Another more common method is by telephone. The criteria in Tribunal Rule 71(1) for non-attendance are limited to "illness, age, incapacity or other sufficient cause" but the decision rests with the hearing Convener to interpret eligibility

(E) Tribunal Rule 61(4)(b). This is unlikely as the onus is on any relevant person to submit a list of witnesses they wish to call. [Tribunal Rule 45(1)(b)] The Tribunal and also any relevant person can formally cite a witness to attend using Tribunal Rule 61(1) but that would involve paying the witness expenses from their own resources under Tribunal Rule 61(4)(b) which again is unlikely.

(F) The MHO may argue for this power to be waived depending on the patient's mental disorder, for example, severe stage of dementia. At the point of writing this book, guidelines have been issued by the Scottish Executive where the MHO can contact the Tribunal to appoint a curator ad litem if the AMP decides the patient is unable to instruct a solicitor.

(G) Section 69; Tribunal Rule 8(2). The MHO may wish to apply for an interim CTO. A common reason may be receiving mental health reports shortly before the short-term certificate expires. The patient/named person too would have insufficient time to seek legal advice. The MHO could submit an incomplete Form CTO 1 and request more time to consult and form a view of the mental health reports as required under section 61(f). This is one of the reasons why a Tribunal is legally obliged to consider an interim CTO before turning to the CTO application itself. The evidence for an interim CTO is the same for a full CTO except the "necessity" test only applies to a shorter period , that is, for up to 56 days. [section 65(6)(b)]

Chapter 4

Reviews and appeal systems

Introduction

- Reviews are built into hospital/community CTOs as a reflection of the principles of minimum restriction and maximum benefit. There are the six–monthly and annual mandatory reviews; also the "from time-to-time" reviews to allow the RMO to check that the legal tests for a CTO are met and that the CTO is necessary.
- The patient's RMO does the review and then refers his decision to the Tribunal. Only the Tribunal can vary the measures in a CTO if an RMO considers that they should be changed.
- The RMO has a legal duty in most types of reviews to consult an MHO who then has specific statutory duties to fulfil to contribute towards these reviews.
- This chapter gives a summary outline of the review system with civil compulsory powers and suggests standard template reports and letters to fulfil that duty.

◆ STAGE 1: Consultation

Who is asking the MHO? What is expected of the MHO?

■ ■ ■ Information points:

There are three types of reviews in civil compulsory powers:

1. On-going review of a short-term detention order [section 49].
2. Mandatory review of a CTO – six-monthly or annual review of an order [section 77 and section 78].
3. On-going review of a CTO (from "time to time" review) [section 80].

1. **On-going review of a short-term detention order** [section 49]
   The MHO has no legal right to be consulted by the RMO about revoking a certificate. The RMO only has to notify the MHO after revoking the certificate.

2. **Mandatory review of a CTO – six-monthly or annual review of an order** [section 77 and section 78]
   There are two types –

   i) the first mandatory review which takes place within six months of a CTO commencing;
   ii) further mandatory reviews – during the next six months and then annually.

   In both types of review, the RMO has to consult the MHO.
   Options for the RMO are fourfold :
   i) revoke the order. [s. 79]
   ii) extend the order by either 6 or 12 months. [s. 86]
   iii) vary the measures in the existing order. [s. 95]
   iv) extend and vary the measures in the order. [s. 90]

3. **On-going review of a CTO (from "time to time" review)** [section 80]
   This can be done at any time in the CTO but should usually be carried out well before the expiry date. If it were carried out within two months of the expiry then the review would change to a mandatory review. The options of a 'from time to time' review are as follows:

   i) revoke the order
   ii) vary the measures in the order under a section 93 application to the Tribunal.

   Note: The RMO is however legally obliged to consult the MHO if he wishes to vary the order as listed above.[1]

MHO – consultation rights:

- The MHO has a statutory right to be consulted by the RMO in the following types of reviews:

   i) First and further mandatory reviews to extend the order. [s. 85]
   ii) Extensions and variations of the order or any recorded matter specified in the order, with all mandatory reviews. [s. 89]
   iii) Variations of measures or any recorded matter specified in the order, in on-going reviews. [s.93(4)(c)]
   iv) RMO applies to Tribunal because a recorded matter is not being provided. [s.96(2)(a)]

- If the MHO disagrees with the extension of a CTO, the Tribunal is legally obliged to convene a hearing.[2]
- If the MHO disagrees with the RMO's decision to extend and vary a CTO, the RMO need only "*have regard to*" the MHO's opinion before making an application to the Tribunal. The Tribunal is also only obliged to give the MHO the opportunity to be heard at a hearing. [s.90(1)(b); s.102 (2)]
- If the MHO disagrees with an RMO's proposal to vary a CTO in an on-going review, again the same legal situation applies as for an extension and variation. [s. 93(4)(c)(i); s. 103(5)]

◆ STAGE 2: Assessment

Information points:

MHO - statutory duties in relation to reviews.
The MHO has statutory duties to fulfil in the following reviews:

1. Extension of a CTO [section 85].
2. Extension and variation of a CTO [section 89].
3. Variation of a CTO [section 95].

1. **Extension of a CTO** [section 85]

RMO chooses to extend a CTO. The RMO has to notify the MHO who has a duty to interview the patient.[3]

- This is called a "section 86 determination" by the RMO. A "determination" is information based on fact and evidence put forward to support it. The RMO therefore includes the views of the MHO as part of the evidence.
- The Act provides for a situation where the MHO is not able to carry out this duty. The Code of Practice suggests the Local Authority allocate another MHO to provide this assessment.[4]

The MHO has the following legal duties towards the patient: [section 85]

i) inform the patient that the RMO is proposing to extend the CTO for either 6 or 12 months;
ii) inform the patient of their rights of appeal;
iii) inform the patient of the availability of independent advocacy services;
iv) to take appropriate steps to ensure the patient has the opportunity to make use of those independent advocacy services.

MHO has to give an opinion on the proposed extension of the CTO.[5]

- The MHO is obliged to inform the RMO whether they disagree with the decision to extend the CTO.
- The MHO should give reasons for either agreeing or disagreeing with this decision.
- If the MHO disagrees with the extension or offers no opinion, or fails to inform the RMO (unlikely), the Tribunal has to hold a hearing.[6]
- The Code of Practice focuses these duties as follows:

i) to inform the patient of their right of appeal under section 99;
ii) to evaluate the effectiveness of the care plan and evaluate how far the objectives are being met;

iii) to assess the extent to which the patient is likely to accept treatment on a voluntary rather than a compulsory basis.[7]

2. Extension and variation of a CTO [section 89][8]

The RMO wishes to extend and vary the CTO. This is called a "section 92 application" to the Tribunal in the Act. The statutory form is called "Form CTO 4"

- The MHO has five duties listed in the Act mainly centred on interviews/ informing the patient of their right of appeal/information-giving of advocacy services and written notification about agreement or disagreement with the extension/and to inform the RMO of any other relevant matters.[9]
- The Act provides for a situation where the MHO is not able to carry out this duty. The Code of Practice suggests the Local Authority allocates another MHO to provide this assessment.[10]
- The Code of Practice advises that the main duty of the MHO is to evaluate the effectiveness of the care plan and evaluate how far the objectives are being met.[11]
- The MHO has the following legal duties towards the patient [section 89]:

  i) inform the patient that the RMO is proposing to extend and vary the CTO for either 6 or 12 months;
  ii) inform the patient of their rights of appeal;
  iii) inform the patient of availability of independent advocacy services;
  iv) to take appropriate steps to ensure the patient has the opportunity to make use of those independent services.

MHO to inform the RMO whether he agrees or disagrees with the extension and variation of the CTO.[12]

- The MHO is obliged to inform the RMO whether they disagree with the decision to extend and vary the CTO.
- The MHO should give reasons for either agreeing or disagreeing with

this proposal although the Act states the MHO only has to give reasons if they disagree with the application.[13]

- The MHO must also inform the RMO of other matters relevant to the application.
- The MHO will have an opportunity to state their opinion at the hearing as only the Tribunal has powers to vary measures.[14]

3. Variation of a CTO [section 95]

MHO has to interview the patient if practicable following notification by the RMO that he wishes to vary the CTO.[15]

- The legal requirement for the MHO to give an opinion on a section 95 application – to vary the CTO – is within the context of other applications, hence the reference to section 92(a)(v). The RMO/MHO duties for varying a CTO are the same. The regulations have modified section 93 of the Act to re-state the same duties.[16]
- The MHO has five duties listed in the Act mainly centred on interviews/informing patient of right of appeal/information-giving of advocacy services and written notification about agreement or disagreement with the extension/and to inform the RMO of any other relevant matters.[17]
- The Code of Practice advises that the main duty of the MHO is to evaluate the effectiveness of the care plan and assess how far the objectives are being met.[18]

MHO to inform the patient of the RMO's section 95 determination and their appeal/advocacy rights.[19]

- The MHO has the following legal duties towards the patient:
  - i) inform the patient that the RMO is proposing to vary the CTO;
  - ii) inform the patient of their rights of appeal;
  - iii) inform the patient of availability of independent advocacy services;
  - iv) to take appropriate steps to ensure the patient has the opportunity to make use of those independent advocacy services.

MHO has to consider opinion on the proposed variation.[20]

- The MHO options are:
  i) MHO can agree or disagree about the variation;
  ii) If the MHO disagrees, they have to state the reasons for this;
  iii) MHO can provide the RMO with any other relevant matters;
  iv) MHO does not have to comply if it is impracticable, for example, they cannot meet the timescales.

- Where situation iv) applies, the Code of Practice suggests the Local Authority allocates another MHO to provide this assessment.[21]
- The MHO must inform the RMO of his decision. This will then trigger the section 95 application by the RMO to vary the CTO.

MHO Report optional to the Tribunal.[22]

The Act gives the Tribunal ancillary powers to request a report from an MHO if there is insufficient information to make a decision about any form of review application. The Regulations have a prescribed format for the MHO when involved with deemed CTOs, that is, those orders imposed by the court before the Act was implemented in October 2005 and CTOs granted by the tribunal hearings[23] (see Practice points below).

The Regulations state that the MHO report should include the following details:

i) on the steps that the Mental Health Officer has taken in pursuance of the requirements imposed by section 85(2)[24] (Mental Health Officer's duties to patient);
ii) giving the views of the Mental Health Officer on the determination and the reasons for those views;
iii) giving, if known to the Mental Health Officer, the views of the patient and the patient's named person on the determination and the reasons for those views;
iv) giving, in so far as the Mental Health Officer considers relevant for the purposes of the review, details of the personal circumstances of the patient;
v) giving, if known to the Mental Health Officer, details of any advance statement that the patient has made (and not

withdrawn); and

vi) giving any other information which the Mental Health Officer considers may assist the Tribunal in considering the determination;

Practice points: MHO report for reviews

- As stated in the Information points above, the Regulations contain prescribed headings an MHO has to use for the different types of reviews. This is in the form of listed headings, much in the same way as for social circumstances reports.
- See Chapter 9 for standard MHO review report to the RMO for compulsory civil reviews. This is combined with the MHO's statutory duty to state whether they agree or disagree with the application. This is in letter form and listed under Stage 3, heading 2. below.

◆ STAGE 3: Notification by MHO

There are three letters which cover the statutory notifications as follows:

1. Standard letter from MHO to the patient informing him of the RMO's proposal; rights of legal representation at the Tribunal; availability of independent advocacy services.
2. Standard letter from the MHO to the RMO re. agreement/ disagreement with the proposal – adapted according to the type of review outlined above.
3. Standard letter to advocacy services re: review.

Note: see Chapter 9 for suggested standard letters.

Information points:

- The MHO only needs to inform the patient and not the named person of the proposal and their appeal rights. It is the duty of the patient's RMO to inform the named person and other parties of the proposal.[25]
- The Tribunal has a legal duty to inform the same list of relevant persons involved with the original CTO application where the RMO is

applying either to vary or to extend and vary the CTO.[(A)]

- If the RMO is only making a determination to extend a CTO, that is, where the criteria in section 101(2) are not met, the Tribunal have no legal duty to inform either the patient or the named person. The Tribunal will instead confirm the RMO's record sent under section 87(2)(b) to the RMO and the MHO.
- The Tribunal will only inform relevant persons if a section 101 hearing has to be held, that is, where there is a change in mental disorder when the CTO was first granted; MHO disagreement with the extension; the CTO has not been reviewed within two years of if being granted.[26]

Additional issues:

Patient/named person appeals to the Tribunal[27]

- The Act allows both patient and named person to appeal a CTO separately.
- There are two types of appeal rights open to a patient/named person:
  i) appeal against an RMO's determination to extend a CTO – section 99.
  The patient and named person can do this at any time after the extension of the CTO begins. However, if refused, they can only appeal again once during the period of the extension.[28]
  ii) appeal to revoke or vary a CTO – section 100.
  The appeal can only be made three months after a CTO is granted. If refused, they can only appeal again once during the period of the extension.
- This is far from clear in the legislation. The built-in restriction is an appeal cannot be made within three months of a CTO being granted or a CTO being reviewed by a Tribunal. The Tribunal reviews are where the CTOs that are extended (s.101) or extended and varied (s.103). The patient and named person can appeal these Tribunal-led CTOs twice in that period, excluding the first three months.[29]
- The same appeal timescales apply to the second 6-month and 12-month periods of the CTO.

- If the Tribunal have not reviewed a CTO, that is, the RMO has only made a section 86 determination with MHO agreement then the patient and named person can appeal at any time. The 3-month restrictions would then start as the Tribunal are now involved with the review.
- The MHO has no statutory duties apart from being given the opportunity to give evidence, orally or in writing, by the Tribunal.[30]

Footnotes:

1 section 95(a); CoP, vol 2, chapter 5, para 8, p. 121.
2 section 101(2)(ii).
3 section 85(2)(a).
4 section 87(2)(a)(iii); CoP, vol 2, chapter 5, para 35, p. 131.
5 section 87(2)(a)(iii).
6 section 101(2)(ii).
7 CoP, vol 2, chapter 5, para 33, p. 131.
8 section 89.
9 section 89(2); CoP, vol 2, chapter 5, para 54, p. 140.
10 section 87(2)(a)(iii); CoP. vol 2, chapter 5, para 56, p. 141.
11 CoP, vol 2, chapter 5, para 55, p. 140.
12 section 89(2)(e).
13 section 89(2)(e)(ii).
14 section 103(5).
15 section 93(4)(c) amended by Scottish Statutory Instrument 2004/No.533 where sections (4A) to (4E) are inserted.
16 Scottish Statutory Instrument 2004. No. 533 inserts subsection (4C) after section 93(4)(c)(i).
17 section 89(2); CoP, vol 2, chapter 5, para 80, p. 151 is cross-referenced to op cit, para 54, p. 140.
18 CoP, op cit, para 55, p. 141.
19 section 93(4)(4C) – see footnote 174 above. Same MHO duties as section 89(2)
20 section 95(a) x-ref: section 92(a)(v).
21 section 87(2)(a)(iii); CoP,vol 2, chapter 5, para 80, p. 151.
22 section 109(2)(b); CoP, vol 2, chapter 5,para 81, p. 152.
23 Scottish Statutory Instrument 2005 No. 366.
24 This reference section will depend on the type of review , that is, section 85(2) – extension of CTO; section 89(2) – extension and variation of CTO; section 93(4)(c)(i) – variation of CTO.
25 section 85(2) MHO only has to inform the patient; section 87(2)(c) RMO informs the patient, named person, MHO and the Mental Welfare Commission.
26 Section 101(2)(b). A Scottish Executive ruling has postponed implementing the review of CTOs until October 2007.
27 section 99 & 100.
28 section 100(7) The patient and named person can appeal separately or together.
29 Notice the appeals do not apply to an RMO's application to vary a CTO (section 95). The patient and named person however can apply to the Tribunal to have the

CTO varied, using section 100(2)(b). This also includes any recorded matter. The RMO has a mandatory duty under section 96 to refer to the Tribunal if a recorded matter is not being met.

30 section 103(5).

Endnotes:

(A) Tribunal Rule 35(1) – notification re: extension of CTO. Tribunal Rule 9(3) – variation/ extension and with variation. Under Tribunal Rule 9(2), the patient and named person also receive a copy of the RMO's section 92/95 applications and a copy of other documents. This would include the MHO's review report.

Chapter 5

Mentally Disordered Persons: Criminal Proceedings

1) Guidance Questions for MHOs

1. What are the main orders?

There are seven main orders related to mentally disordered offenders. See reference below for each order.

i) **Assessment order**
– 28 days at the pre-conviction stage.

ii) **Treatment order**
– any detention period pre-conviction stage.

iii) **Interim compulsion order**
– initially 3 months then reviewed every three months up to 12 months. Post-conviction, pre-disposal.

iv) **Compulsion order**
– starts at 6 months. Final disposal.

v) **Compulsion order with a restriction order [CORO]**

vi) **Transfer for treatment direction**
– any time during the sentence period.

vii) **Hospital direction**
– at the start of the sentence period.

2. What are the key MHO duties?

Duty 1

Social circumstances report [section 231]

- The key duty is to prepare a social circumstances report after each order is made. The Act terms these orders as a "*relevant event*". They are orders listed above except for COROs.
- The MHO can dispense with preparing an SCR if they consider an SCR would serve little, or no, practical purpose. If this were the case, the MHO would have to state those reasons in the section headed "*Requirement for SCR*", text box 1 of Form SCR 1 (see Chapter 8 for details of SCR preparation for each order).

Duty 2

Compulsion order [section 133, subsection 57C, p. 105]

- The Act says "*if directed to do so by the court, the MHO shall prepare a report*"
- For guidance on the MHO report see Code of Practice volume 3, Part 1, chapter 5, paragraph 32-44, pp. 130-132.

Duty 3

Identify a named person [section 250]

- This applies with three orders:
  i) Compulsion order
  ii) CORO
  iii) Hospital direction

Note: see Chapter 7 for detailed guidance on named person.

- The MHO has a set of duties in each of the following reviews, not least in giving an opinion as to whether they agree or disagree with the review.

Duty 4

Consultation about reviews to extend and/or vary a compulsion order

This is similar to reviewing CTOs except the first 6-month review is before a tribunal hearing.

Duty 5

Consultation for compulsion order with a restriction order

This is an annual review by the RMO.

Duty 6

Contribution to the medical assessment before a transfer for treatment direction [TTD] is made by the Scottish Ministers

The Scottish Ministers decide on the medical request for a TTD. There is no legal requirement for the RMO to consult the MHO before making this recommendation. The Code of Practice, however, suggests it would be "*good practice*" for an MHO to contribute to the medical assessment.[1]

Duty 7

Contribution to the medical assessment before the court makes a hospital direction

The court requires an MHO report under section 59B of the 1995 Act before imposing a hospital direction.

2) Details of the MHO duties

Duty 1

Social circumstances report for the following orders [section 231(1)]

Standard MHO requirements for all the Orders:

- The MHO has to provide an SCR within 21 days of an Order being imposed.
- There is a standard form issued by the Scottish Executive, which can be used for this purpose. The form has a selection of 19 listed factors on the personal circumstances of the patient for the MHO to comment on where relevant and appropriate.[2]
- The purpose of this SCR is to contribute to the mental health assessment of the person and consider if further orders are required.
- Copies of the SCR should be sent to the patient's RMO and the Mental Welfare Commission. This should be recorded on Form SCR 1.

i) **Assessment order**

– 28-day assessment order imposed by the court[3]

- The purpose of an assessment order is to allow the assessment and treatment of a person who is awaiting either trial or sentence in a hospital by a Psychiatrist. This can last for up to 28 days but is usually less to allow time for a final disposal, for example, a compulsion order where two medical reports and possibly an MHO report has to be completed before the 28th day in order to keep the patient in hospital. There is no right of appeal.

ii) **Treatment order** made by the court[4]

- A treatment order detains a person in a hospital awaiting trial or sentence.
- The treatment order ends after the court has passed sentence.
- There is no right of appeal in a treatment order.

Details: The purpose of this SCR is to contribute to the mental health assessment as follows:

a) what are the elements of any on-going care and treatment plans?
b) are appropriate services available?
c) are compulsory powers appropriate?
d) identify and detail the powers of compulsion required.

iii) Interim compulsion order made by court
[section 131; subsection 53(2), p. 95]

- An interim compulsion order is used where the court is thinking of imposing a compulsion order with a restriction order or a hospital direction.[5]
- It can be renewed for 12 weeks at a time, up to a maximum of 52 weeks.
- The purpose of the order is to allow for a prolonged period of in-patient assessment before a final disposal is made for mentally disordered offenders who have committed a serious offence and/or appear to pose a considerable risk to themselves or others.

Details: The purpose of this SCR is to contribute to the mental health assessment as follows:

a) do the circumstances of the case require consideration of a restriction order?
b) do the circumstances of the case require consideration of a hospital direction?

iv) Compulsion order made by the court
[section 133, subsection 57A(2), p. 101]

- A compulsion order is broadly similar to a CTO in that the patient can receive medical treatment either in hospital or in the community.
- Once a court grants a compulsion order, they cannot pass any other sentences[6]. This is seen as a mental health disposal for an offender, hence the use of lengthy assessments in complex cases, for example, Interim compulsion orders that can last up to one year.
- The main differences from a CTO are:

a) there is no criterion for the patient making decisions about their treatment.[7]

b) the person has committed an offence punishable by imprisonment, excluding murder.[8]

c) the court has no power to specify any treatment, care or service as a "*recorded matter*" in the compulsion order.[9]

d) the court should be satisfied this is the most viable alternative to the other sentencing options available.[10]

Social circumstances report – details.

- The requirements of this SCR should mirror those for a CTO.
- The Code of Practice suggests the various parties of the patient's multi-disciplinary team should carry out the following duties:[11]
  a) reviewing the need for the order;
  b) reviewing whether or not the principles are being respected;
  c) keeping the care plan under review.

v) Compulsion order with a restriction order
[section 59 of the 1995 Act]

- The combination of compulsion order and restriction order is referred to as a CORO.
- Adding a restriction order may be recommended in a case where a mentally disordered offender appears to pose a significant risk of serious harm to any other person. The aim is to ensure adequate protection of the public as the offender goes through rehabilitation.
- The person must be treated in a secure environment. A restriction order will therefore only be made in addition to a hospital based compulsion order; it can not be made with community based orders. The order will set out the specific hospital secure unit which is to be used.
- Adding a restriction order means that the measures specified in the compulsion order will then be without limit of time. This has the effect of putting the offender under unlimited detention.
- There are safeguards in that the Tribunal must review the compulsion order and restriction order at a minimum of every two years.
- The making of the restriction order would require that the court be satisfied that:

- the *nature* of the offence,
- the *antecedents* of the person, and
- the risk that as a result of the mental disorder the person would commit *offences* if set at large,
- it is necessary to make the restriction order for the *protection* of the public from *serious harm*.

- In a case where a mentally disordered offender appears to pose such a significant risk to others that consideration is being given to making a CORO, therefore, it would be normal for an *interim compulsion order* [under s. 53 CPSA] to be made first.

vi)(a) Transfer for treatment direction [section 136(2)]

- A transfer for treatment direction (TTD) allows for the transfer of a prisoner during his sentence who has become mentally ill for treatment in a hospital.
- The transfer is decided by the Scottish Ministers and not the court, as the prisoner has already been sentenced. Time spent in hospital counts towards time served against the sentence.
- The prisoner automatically becomes a restricted patient while the TTD order lasts.
- There must be two medical reports recommending this transfer, one of which must come from an AMP.[12]
- The prisoner can also be transferred to the State Hospital if there is sufficient level of risk posed to others.[13]
- The prisoner cannot refuse medical treatment.

vi)(b) MHO contribution to this assessment

- The Code of Practice suggests the MHO should be involved with the medical practitioner at the outset of the assessment even though there is no legal requirement to complete any report.
- The MHO should address the following issues:[14]
    i) the views of the prisoner about the proposed transfer;
    ii) the views of the prison staff;
    iii) the medical concerns about the prisoner's mental health;

iv) the diagnosis and proposed treatment;
v) consider alternative ways to avoid compulsory powers;
vi) assess the risks if the prisoner were not made subject of compulsory powers.

vi) (c) Social circumstances report following the transfer of a prisoner for hospital treatment[15]

Additional note: There is no direct legal reference to an SCR in section 136 but it is regarded as a *"relevant event"* under section 232 (b)(viii).

vii) Hospital direction

[section 59A of the Criminal Procedure (Scotland) Act 1995]

- The hospital direction was inserted into the 1995 Act by amendments made in the Crime and Punishment (Scotland) Act 1997.
- A hospital direction under section 59A of the 1995 Act allows the court to have a convicted person receive treatment in a hospital. When the treatment is complete, the person ('prisoner') would be transferred to the prison to complete their custodial sentence.
- The suspension and/or transfer procedures mirror those of a CORO.

Social circumstances report following a hospital direction

Note: There is no direct legal reference to an SCR in section 136 but it is regarded as a "*relevant event*" under section 232(b)(vii).

- The Code of Practice states that best practice would suggest the MHO send a copy of the SCR to the Scottish Ministers.[16]

Note: 1. If the patient continues to need medical treatment after the custodial sentence has expired, the 'direction' ceases to have effect. The MHO would need to apply to the Tribunal for a CTO using the wording in Schedule 3 of the 2003 Act as applied to the Tribunal powers. This allows the Tribunal to make a CTO within 28 days of the hospital direction expiring.[17]

2. The Code of Practice suggests using an emergency and/or short-term detention certificate would be a rare occurrence.[18]
3. For further reference on the MHO duties see the Code of Practice, volume 3, Part 2, chapter 8, paras 06-09, p. 299-300.

Duty 2

MHO's court report before a compulsion order is made [section 133, subsection 57C, page 105]

- The Act states the court has discretion to request a report from an MHO] *"if directed to do so by the court, the MHO shall..."* [19]
- The Scottish Executive have issued a directive dated 25.01.06. stating the courts must request an MHO report in every case where a compulsion order is being considered.
- There is also a comprehensive pro-forma for an MHO report available from their website address: www.scotland.gov.uk/Resource/Doc/ 924/0021075.doc
- This report gives specific guidance assessment points to include in the MHO report for compulsion orders; restriction orders; hospital direction.
- The report must include the following information: [20]

  i) the name and address of the person;
  ii) the name and address of the offender's primary carer, if known;
  iii) details of any personal circumstances of the offender relevant to the psychiatric recommendations for a compulsion order;
  iv) any other information the MHO considers relevant to the recommendations for a compulsion order.

- The MHO should consider the following matters: [21]

i) the personal circumstances of the offender relevant to the recommendation for a compulsion order;
ii) the views of the primary carer and the named person where known;
iii) the MHO's opinion on the suitability and viability of the powers being sought in the compulsion order;
iv) unlike a CTO, the MHO does not have to prepare a proposed care plan. The RMO must do this after the CO is made [section 137(2)];
v) confirmation that any community services that are to form part of the compulsion order are suitable and available;
vi) a description of any alternative mental health disposals that in all circumstances of the case could be considered by the court;
vii) if the MHO thinks alternatives to a mental health disposal are feasible they may advise the court to request a Social Enquiry Report to assess the viability of these alternatives.[22]

Duty 3

Identify a named person [Section 250]

This role applies with three orders –

i) Compulsion order [section 138];
ii) Compulsion order with a restriction order [section 181(2)];
iii) Hospital direction [section 205(2)].

- The Act states the MHO must "*take such steps as are reasonably practicable to ascertain the name and address of the patient's named person*." (see Chapter 7 for guidance on named persons).

Duty 4

Consultation about reviews to extend and/or vary a compulsion order

There are four types of reviews as follows:

i) First review – to extend the compulsion order [section 148].
ii) Further reviews – to extend the compulsion order [section 150].
iii) RMO's determination to extend and vary a compulsion order [section 154].
iv) RMO's *"from time to time"* review to vary a compulsion order [section 159].

Details:

i) First review – to extend the compulsion order [section 148]

The MHO's duties are similar to the CTO review for an extension. They are as follows:

- Section 146(2) requires the RMO to consult the MHO as part of a proposal to extend a first review.
- The RMO then has to apply to the Tribunal to extend the compulsion order under section 149 and record within the application Form CTO 3a whether or not the MHO agrees with the proposed extension.[23]
- The Code of Practice advises the main duties of the MHO are to evaluate the effectiveness of the care plan and evaluate how far the objectives are being met.[24]
- The MHO has the following legal information-giving duties towards the patient: [25]
  i) the RMO is proposing to extend the CO for 6 or 12 months;[26]
  ii) their rights of legal representation at reviews;
  iii) the availability of independent advocacy services;
  iv) to take appropriate steps to ensure the patient has the opportunity to make use of those independent services

Note: see Chapter 9 for notification letters as follows:

a) Letter 1 MHO to patient reference CO review.
b) Letter 2 MHO to RMO reference views on the application[27] and an MHO report for the Tribunal.[28]
c) Letter 3 MHO to Advocacy Services reference the application.[29]

ii) Further reviews to extend a compulsion order [section 150]

- The MHO duties are similar to those of section 147(2) above (see Letters in Chapter 9).
- The RMO still needs to consult the MHO for their views under section 150(2). If the MHO agrees with the 12-month extension there is no tribunal hearing.
- A tribunal hearing must be convened if the MHO disagrees with the RMO's proposed extension; if there is a change in mental disorder; or if the CO has not been reviewed within two years of the original order.[30]

iii) RMOs determination to extend and vary a compulsion order [section 154]

- The MHO duties are similar to those of section 147(2) (see Letters in Chapter 9).
- The Tribunal must hold a hearing regardless of whether or not the MHO agrees with the compulsion order where the RMO is applying to vary and/or extend the CO.[31]

iv) RMOs *"from time to time"* review to vary a compulsion order [section 159]

- The RMO only needs to consult the MHO about their views on varying a compulsion order.
- The MHO has no formal legal duties to interview the patient or formally notify the RMO of their opinion but the Code of Practice makes a cross-reference to the MHO role for CTOs under section 89(2)(e), that is, a "*time to time*" review.[32]

- The MHO has five duties listed in the Act mainly centred on interviews/informing the patient of right of appeal/information-giving of advocacy services and written notification about agreement or disagreement with the extension/and to inform the RMO of any other relevant matters[33] (see Letters in Chapter 9).
- The Tribunal must allow the MHO, as well as other relevant parties, the opportunity to be heard before varying a compulsion order.[34]

Duty 5

Reviewing a compulsion order and restriction order (abbreviated to: CORO) [1995 Act section 59(1)][35]

Summary information on reviews of COROs

- This is where a court decides at the disposal stage to impose a restriction order along with a compulsion order. The criteria for special restrictions are set out in Part 10 of the Act.[36]
- A CORO is not time-limited and therefore does not need to be renewed. It is reviewed, however, in a similar way to a compulsion order.[37]
- The CORO review also contains the legal test "to *protect any other person from serious harm.... whether or not for medical treatment*" under section 182(3)(b)(ii). For this reason, a shrieval panel formally reviews the CORO at least every two years under section 189.[38]
- Suspension of the measures or transfer to another hospital by the RMO must be authorised by the Scottish Ministers.
- However, a shrieval panel has the power to revoke a CORO and to decide on the conditional or absolute discharge of a patient.[39]

Shrieval panel: [2003 Act, Schedule 2, Part 1, para 2, page 249]

- This is still a Tribunal panel – not court-based – with a sheriff, sheriff principal or a part-time sheriff, re-named as "*sheriff conveners*". The wing members would be medical and general as in Tribunal panels for CTOs.

- The shrieval panel would be convened wherever the patient was being treated, for example, in a state hospital, local hospital or if already conditionally discharged, in a location near their home.
- If the CORO is changed and the person is transferred from, say, the state hospital or a medium secure hospital to another (local) hospital, then further reviews will be convened in the local area as the patient is effectively now discharged from the first hospital.
- Patients may be conditionally discharged for an indefinite period but are subject to recall to hospital by the Scottish Ministers during this period.[40]
- The RMO must consult the designated MHO for their views in advance of making any recommendation to the Scottish Ministers for a change to be made in the status of the patient.[41] [(A)]
- The Scottish Ministers have a duty to refer patients to the Tribunal to be heard by a shrieval panel if they receive a recommendation from an RMO or the Mental Welfare Commission.[42] This effectively means all professional assessments about restriction orders have to be administered by the Scottish Ministers who then refer the recommendation to the Tribunal.[43]
- The patient and the patient's named person may make applications directly to the Tribunal but there are timescales that prohibit an application, that is, six months from the beginning of the compulsion order and 3 months for any Tribunal review decisions stemming from the RMO/Commission/Scottish Ministers/patient/patient's named person.[44]

Best practice summary points for the MHO when reviewing a CORO[45]

When forming his/her opinion in relation to the annual review of a patient subject to a CORO [section 182(3)(c)] the MHO should:

- interview the patient;
- consult the named person and relatives/carer/significant other;
- consult the RMO;
- consult all members of the multi-disciplinary team where relevant and appropriate;

- review medical and social work records;
- with the patient's agreement, consult any other relevant person who is significantly involved in the patient's care and treatment.

Best practice summary points for the MHO when consulted by the RMO about a CORO[46]

Although not set down in the Act best practice would suggest that when forming an opinion in relation to the review of a CORO, some of the issues that the MHO should consider may include:

- Does the patient continue to suffer from a mental disorder?
- What is the psychiatric opinion and evidence in relation to this matter?
- Does the patient require medical treatment in a hospital?
- Could the treatment be provided safely and effectively in the community?
- As a result of the mental disorder does the patient present a risk of serious harm to others?
- Which compulsory measures are necessary to safeguard the patient's care and treatment requirements, and ensure the safety of others?

Duty 6

Transfer for treatment direction [TTD] – contribution to the medical assessment for the Scottish Ministers

- The Scottish Ministers decide on the medical recommendation for a TTD from prison to a hospital and not the court. There is no legal requirement for the RMO to consult the MHO before making this recommendation.
- The Code of Practice, however, suggests it would be "*best practice*" for an MHO to contribute to the medical assessment.[47]

Duty 7

Hospital direction – MHO duty to prepare a court report

- The MHO must prepare a court report under section 59B of the 1995 Act.
- The contents of this report are similar to a compulsion order and a CORO.
- The key difference is the offender – person just sentenced – cannot be treated in the community.
- The Code of Practice states the MHO must consider an alternative disposal such as a CORO or no hospital treatment at all. This would be rare given the MHO has firstly to seek the views of the clinical team treating the person. Much of this assessment would have been done while the person was detained under an interim compulsion order given this is the prerequisite for a hospital direction disposal.[48]

Note: The MHO consultation for reviews of both a TTD and a hospital direction are the same. These reviews should be done along the same lines as for compulsion orders.[49]

Footnotes:

1 CoP, vol. 3, Part 2, chapter 5, paras 16-19, p. 263.
2 Form SCR 1. See CoP, vol. 1, chapter 11, para 4, p. 161 for details on the content of an SCR.
3 section 130, subsection 52D(2), p. 80.
4 section 130, subsection 52M(2), p. 88.
5 section 131, subsection 53(6), p. 96.
6 section 133 ss57A(15)(a), p. 104 lists the seven available disposals excluded to the court after a compulsion order has been made.
7 Compare with section 64(5)(d) for a CTO where the patient's decision-making about medical treatment is significantly impaired.
8 section 133, subsection 57A(1)(a), p. 101.
9 The Code of Practice however recommends the RMO draw up a care plan along the lines of a recorded matter. This should be included in the statutory care plan under section 137(2). CoP, vol 3, Part 2, chapter 1, para 04, p. 201.
10 section 133, subsection 57A(4)(c), p. 101.
11 CoP, vol 2, chapter 4, para 25, p. 107. This is cross-referenced with CoP, vol. 3, Part 2, chapter 6, para 23, p. 273.

12 section 136(2).
13 section 136 (5).
14 CoP, vol 3, Part 2, chapter 6, para 25, p. 273.
15 section 231(1).
16 CoP, vol 3, Part 2, chapter 6, para 23, p. 273.
17 Schedule 3, para 2, p. 256.
18 CoP, vol 3, Part 2, chapter 8 para 08, p. 299.
19 section 133, ss. 57C(2), p. 105.
20 section 133, subsection 57C(4) p.105.
21 CoP, vol 3, Part 1, chapter 5, para 38, p. 131.
22 CoP, vol 3, Part 1, chapter 6, paras 108-112, pp. 193-4.
23 section 149(a)(iii).
24 CoP, vol 2, chapter 5, para 33, p. 131. Note: the CoP volume for reviewing a compulsion order is cross-referenced with the same procedures for a CTO. There is a table of cross-references on CoP, vol 3, Part 2, chapter 1, pp. 213-216. Not easy to follow.
25 section 147(2)(b).
26 Note: The first review is a 6-month extension granted by a Tribunal under 167(1)(a); the further reviews to extend can be done by the RMO for up to 12 month periods – section 152(1). This is called a "determination" similar to CTO extensions under section 86.
27 section 147(2)(d) – agree or disagree with the CO and any other relevant matters.
28 section 173(1) The Tribunal have ancillary powers to request an MHO report where there is insufficient information to make a decision . The relevant regulation in section 173(2) (b) which prescribes this MHO report is Scottish Statutory Instrument 2005 No. 365.
29 section 147(2)(c) – this is evidence the MHO has been proactive in giving the patient the use of an independent advocacy services under section 259 of the Act.
30 section 165(2) (a) & (b). Note: The section 165(2)(b) reviews will come into effect from October 2007.
31 section 158 – extending and varying the CO; section 161(a) – varying the CO.
32 Code of Practice, vol 3, Part 2, chapter 1, p. 213 x-ref. with CoP, vol 2, chapter 5, para 13, p. 123.
33 section 89(2)(e); guidance for this duty is x-ref with CoP, vol 2, chapter 5, paras 54-56, pp. 140-1.
34 section 167(6) which x-references to section 166(3)(e).
35 Note: The court makes a CORO using the 1995 Act but the subsequent reviews are dealt with in the 2003 Act, that is, Part 10, pp. 130-143.
36 For a summary of a CORO, see CoP, vol 3, Part 2, paras 03 to 12, pp. 219-220.
37 One main difference between a compulsion order and a CORO is the review is done by the RMO only on an annual basis. The "*time to time*" reviews for both orders remain the same – section 184 (2).
38 This review process is being implemented for all COROs in Scotland from October 2006.
39 section 193 – extensive wording with ten subsections.
40 section 202(2) following conditional discharge by the Tribunal under section 193(7).
41 section 182(3)(c). The RMO need only "*have regard*" to the MHO's views before submitting his report to the Scottish Ministers under section 183(6). The MHO has the opportunity to lead evidence at the Tribunal stage under section 193(8).
42 section185 (1) – RMO; section 187(2) – Mental Welfare Commission.
43 CoP, vol 3, Part 2, chapter 3, para 12, p. 233.
44 section 192(4). This is x-ref to section 193, that is, references to the Tribunal via

the Scottish Ministers.

45 CoP, vol 3, Part 2, chapter 3, para 22, p. 237 – direct extract from the Code of Practice.

46 CoP, vol 3, Part 2, para 24, p. 237 – direct extract from the Code of Practice.

47 CoP, vol 3, Part 2, paras 16-19, p. 263. Paragraph 18 lists six useful assessment points for an MHO to consider before giving their agreement.

48 section 131, subsection 53(6), p. 96; CoP, vol 3, Part 1, chapter 5, paras 116-121, p. 150.

49 section 206(3)(c)(i); CoP, vol 3, Part 2, chapter 7, paras 24-26, p. 289.

Endnote:

(A) Section 183(4); CoP, vol 3, Part 2, chapter 3, para 01, p. 228 sets out the review criteria which the RMO must use as a basis for making a recommendation. Furthermore, the Code later advises in paragraph 04 "*it would be expected that he/she would be fully supported by all members of the multi-disciplinary team who are involved in providing care, support and treatment to the patient*". This means the MHO should take individual views into account before giving a view.

Chapter 6

Warrants

Some headings in this chapter are in a question-answer style to help the MHO work through essential information before going to court. All the 16 statutory forms in the warrant procedure are detailed. There are also two sample forms for a section 35 and section 293 applications. Some practice tips are inserted where applicable.

1) Introduction

- The MHO has a unique role within the Act in applying for warrants or a removal order. The MHO is the only professional who can do this with the exception of a section 292 warrant where the MHO can share this responsibility with another authorised person.[A]
- A warrant is issued on application either to a sheriff court where the person subject to the warrant lives, or the justice of the peace [termed: "justice"].[B] Both sheriff and the justice have to hear evidence before granting the warrant.
- Both a warrant and an order allow a constable to open lockfast premises.
- See below for the legal difference between a warrant and an order.

Warrant [section 35 and 292]

A warrant:

(i) allows access and investigation (section 35);
(ii) allows an MHO and others to enter the premises of a detained patient who has absconded from the place specified in the original order and is refusing access (locked door) [section 292];
(iii) allows an authorised person to bring into custody a patient who is non-compliant with treatment and requires hospital assessment (section 113).

The warrant only allows the use of force by a constable to open the lockfast premises.[1] Further use of "*reasonable force*" under section 303(6) to return a patient to hospital is sanctioned only for a patient absconding and not for a patient returned to custody under section 113(4).

Order [section 293 and 294]

An order applies to any person who has a mental disorder to be removed from their premises and taken to a place of safety for up to 7 days.[2] The evidence for an order is more stringent. The person also has a right to be heard before a sheriff grants the order.

- Section 35 warrants do not distinguish the granting authority between a sheriff and the justice. A removal order, however, has separate sections in the Act for the powers of a sheriff and a justice of the peace.[3]
- The main difference is there are no rights to appeal against a justice of the peace's decision to grant or refuse an order. The person subject to a removal order can only later apply to the sheriff to have the order revoked or varied.[4]
- Section 294 therefore advises an application to a justice should only be made where a court application is impracticable and urgent. This is likely to happen out of court hours or when a sheriff is not available during court hours. Local practice across Scotland's 49 sheriff courts varies.
- Lay justices are appointed within their commission area in Scotland.[5] They are currently trained and given legal advice by the Clerk of the District Court who is employed by the local authority. The MHO should therefore check the protocol for contacting a justice of the peace and whether or not a clerk of court or a deputy clerk of court should be present while evidence from the MHO is heard.[(C)]

2) Warrants

a) Section 35 Warrant – Warrant to enter premises

◆ What is it?

There are three separate warrants an MHO can use as follows:[6]

i) enter a person's premises by force where refusal has taken place or refusal is likely to take place, or perhaps where there is no response.
ii) allow a medical practitioner to examine the person for up to three hours on the premises.
iii) allow a medical practitioner to obtain access to a person's medical records when that person is unable to give consent.

- The MHO may want to apply for all three warrants at the same time to cover the circumstances of the person or use them individually according to the nature of the inquiry under section 33.

◆ When might a Warrant be used?

- These are specified in section 33 where a local authority has a duty to inquire into the circumstances of any person over 16 years of age as follows.[7] The person "appears" to have a mental disorder and may be, or may have been subject, or exposed to –
    - i) ill-treatment;
    - ii) neglect; or
    - iii) some other deficiency in care or treatment.[8]
- Other circumstances: because of the mental disorder the person's property –
    - i) may be suffering, or may have suffered, loss or damage; or
    - ii) may be, or may have been, at risk of suffering loss or damage.[9]
- The person may be –
    - i) living alone without care; and
    - ii) unable to look after him/herself or his/her property or financial affairs.[10]

- Finally, because of the mental disorder, the safety of some other person may be at risk.[11]

◆ Who is involved?

- The MHO has to give evidence before either a sheriff or a justice of the peace who then decides whether to grant the warrant.
- The MHO can cite specific names in the warrant to accompany him into the person's house, for example, a General Practitioner (GP) or community psychiatric nurse (CPN).
- The MHO can then use the warrant to allow any constable to open lockfast premises of the person named in the warrant.

◆ How long will the Warrant last?

Warrant 1: section 35(2) – open lockfast premises – 8 days.
Warrant 2: section 35(4) – medical examination – 3 hours.
Warrant 3: section 35(7) – access to the person's medical records – unspecified.

◆ Who is expected to cooperate?

The Act makes it clear the following agencies shall comply with a request from the local authority for assistance:[12]

i) the Mental Welfare Commission.[13]
ii) the Public Guardian.[14]
iii) the Scottish Commission for the Regulation of Care.[15]
iv) Health Board.
v) the National Health Service trust.

◆ Can the person subject to the Warrant appeal?

No. This also applies to any interested parties.[16]

◆ What is likely to happen after the Warrant has been issued?

- The warrant does not allow a person to be removed from their premises. To do this, the person would need to be formally detained from that premises using civil compulsory powers. They would then be taken to a hospital as a detained patient on either an emergency or short-term detention certificate.
- The alternative would be to remove that person to a place of safety for up to 7 days using a removal order. This could be a hospital, a care home or any other suitable place as defined in the Act[17] (see removal order section 293 below for further details).

◆ What are the MHO duties after the Warrant has been granted or refused?

The MHO has to write to the Mental Welfare Commission to inform them as to whether or not the application has been granted or refused.[18]

b) Section 293 – removal order

◆ What is it?

- This is an order allowing the removal of a person from their premises to a "place of safety" which can be a hospital, a care home or any other suitable place as defined in section 300 of the Act.
- There are statutory forms available online (see below for details on each form).

◆ When might an order be used?

- These are specified in section 293(2) where an MHO has given evidence to a sheriff into the circumstances of anyone over the age of 16. The sheriff or justice of the peace have to be satisfied that the person has a mental disorder and is subject, or exposed, to:
    - i) ill-treatment;
    - ii) neglect; or
    - iii) some other deficiency in care or treatment.[19]

- Other circumstances: because of the mental disorder the person's property:

  i) may be suffering, or may have suffered, loss or damage; or
  ii) may be, or may have been, at risk of suffering loss or damage.[20]

- The person who has a mental disorder may be:

  i) living alone or without care; and
  ii) unable to look after him/herself or his/her property or financial affairs.[21]

- Finally, that person is likely to suffer significant harm if not removed to a place of safety.[22]

Note: Given the specific wording in the Act quoted above, a medical practitioner should confirm in advance with the MHO that the person has a mental disorder. The MHO may wish to have the medical practitioner present as a witness (see below). This differs from section 35 warrants where the MHO only has to suspect the person may have a mental disorder, that is, the wording is "*where it appears to a local authority.*"[23]

◆ Who is involved?

- The MHO has to give evidence before either a sheriff or a justice of the peace who then decides whether to grant the order. This can be done orally but it would be preferable for the MHO to use the statutory Forms MHO 5 or MHO 6.
- The MHO can cite specific names in the order to accompany him into the house, for example, a GP to confirm the diagnosis of mental disorder, CPN or a community care provider who may be used for the place of safety.
- The MHO can then use the order to allow any police constable to open lockfast premises of the person named in the warrant.

◆ How long will the Warrant last?

- The order to enter any lockfast premises lasts for 72 hours from the time the warrant was signed.[24]
- The order authorises the removal of the person cited to be held in a place of safety for up to 7 days.[25]

◆ Who is expected to cooperate?

- The main agency would be the police.
- A medical practitioner or a care home provider may also be involved to assess the person's suitability for a specific place of safety. The medical practitioner may consider using civil compulsory powers to admit the person to a hospital if specific treatment is required.
- The evidence has to prove the person has a mental disorder before a removal order can be granted. This could be confirmed by using a section 35(4) warrant where a medical practitioner has examined the person in their home or if the person has been recently examined by a medical practitioner. The person subject to the order can legally oppose this assessment (see below).

◆ Can the person subject to the order be heard before the warrant is granted?

- Yes. The person subject to the order is entitled to be heard either orally or in writing and to lead or produce evidence.[26] This also applies to the following parties[27]:
  i) the person's nearest relative;[28]
  ii) any guardian of the person;[(D)]
  iii) any welfare attorney of the person;[(E)]
  iv) the person's primary carer.[(F)]

- The sheriff can dispense with this right to be heard if he considers such a delay would be prejudicial to the subject of the application.[29] If appropriate, the MHO should provide evidence of this with the application. The most obvious one would be threat of abuse from another person, hence the need for the warrant.

◆ Can a justice of the peace grant an order?

Yes. If access to a sheriff is impracticable or any delays would be prejudicial to the subject of the application.[(G)] In this instance, however, there is no right for the person named in the order or any relevant parties to be heard before the order is granted. That appeal right to have the order revoked or varied only applies after the warrant is signed.

◆ Can the warrant be recalled or varied?

- Yes. The person in the order or any relevant parties listed above can apply to the sheriff only and not to the justice of the peace, to have the removal order either:
    - i) recalled, that is, suspended or cancelled; or
    - ii) varying that order by –
        - a) specifying a different place of safety before the warrant expires;
        - b) authorising the removal to this different place of safety;) and
        - c) authorising the detention of the person in this new place of safety for the remainder of the 72 hour period.[30]

- If the removal order is recalled, the sheriff can make an order authorising the person to be returned to the place they were moved from or to another place of their choice.[31]

◆ Can the order be appealed once made?

No. Neither a 7-day order nor a recalled/varied order can be appealed.

◆ What is likely to happen after the Warrant has been issued?

- The person cited in the order will be removed by a police constable and taken to a place of safety.
- This has to be to done within 72 hours of the warrant being granted by either the sheriff or the justice of the peace.

- The person cited in the order can be kept in this place of safety for up to 7 days, which means the day the warrant was granted, plus 6 calendar days.
- This will allow time for further assessment by a medical practitioner and an MHO to decide on any compulsory orders in the Act or the use of the Adults with Incapacity (Scotland) Act 2000, for example, a Guardianship Order.
- The Code of Practice suggests a person should be moved on from a place of safety to a more suitable care and treatment environment as "*quickly as is safe and practical.*" [32]
- A Care Programme Approach meeting could be convened as an alternative to legal measures while the person is allowed to return home.

◆ What are the MHO duties after the order has been granted or refused?

- There are no legal requirements for an MHO to inform the Mental Welfare Commission of this order and the circumstances and results which led to it (compare to a section 35 warrant above).
- The MHO does not have to inform the person cited in the order or any relevant parties of their right of appeal to recall or vary the order under section 295.
- The Code of Practice however suggests this would be best practice if the MHO carried out these two duties.[33]

3) Warrants forms

Summary points[34]

- There are 16 forms in total. Below is a summary of the forms for reference. The reason why there are so many forms is that there are three separate warrant applications under section 35:
    - i) to enter premises;
    - ii) to allow a person to be medically examined for up to 3 hours;
    - iii) to allow access to a person's medical records.

- Each application is completed and signed by an MHO. There are, therefore, three warrants issued which the sheriff or a justice of the peace signs.
- The same reasons apply to sections 292/293/294, that is, application and signed warrant, either by a sheriff or a justice (separate warrants). The justice of the peace's warrant is not appealable, hence the reason why it is a separate warrant.

Form MH01

Application form for warrant entering premises under section 35(1)
This is completed and signed by the MHO. The Application can be made to either a sheriff or a justice of the peace.

Form MH01A

Warrant form under section 35(1) – warrant to enter premises
The sheriff or a justice of the peace signs this.

Form MH02

Application form for warrant detaining a person under section 35(4) for the purpose of enabling a medical examination
This is completed and signed by the MHO. The Application can be made to either a sheriff or a justice of the peace.

Form MH02A

Warrant under section 35(4) to detain a person for the purposes of enabling a medical examination
The sheriff or the justice of the peace would sign this.

Form MH03

Application form for warrant for access to medical records under section 35(7)
Completed and signed by an MHO. The application can be made to either a sheriff or a justice of the peace.

Form MH03A

Warrant under section 35(7) – warrant for access to medical records
A sheriff or a justice of the peace signs this warrant.

Form MH04

Application form for warrant to enter premises under section 292
This can be signed and completed by either an MHO or another prescribed person, for example, a nurse/doctor. It is for a person already detained under the 2003 Act who is refusing access in order to be returned to the hospital. The application can be made to either a sheriff or a justice of the peace.

Form MH04A

Warrant under section 292(1)
Either a sheriff or a justice of the peace can sign this warrant to return a detained patient to hospital.

Form MH05

Application form for removal order under section 293(1)
This is to remove a non-detained person who is known to have a mental disorder and is refusing access. It is completed and signed only by an MHO. The MHO can either state the names of any person who should be notified in order to make an appeal or state his/her reasons for the sheriff to waive those intimations (notifications).
This application can only be lodged in the Sheriff Court. The reason for

this is that the person subject to the warrant has a right of appeal, which only the sheriff can hear.

Form MH05A

Form of intimation of application for removal order under section 293(1)

This is to allow the person subject to the order and any other interested parties the opportunity to appeal the order to have them removed from their home to a place of safety for up to 7 days [section 293(5).

It is completed by the sheriff clerk and sent to the person subject to the order and any interested parties. It informs them of the place/date/time of the appeal.

Form MH05B

Removal order under section 293(3)

It is signed by the sheriff and specifies the names of the people who are to accompany the MHO to carry out the order. The police constable is not named but instead there is a section to include the name of his/her police force.

Form MH06

Application form to justice of the peace for removal order under section 294

Completed and signed by an MHO. This form is only used if it is impracticable to obtain access to a sheriff. It has the same authority as a removal order signed by a sheriff although it cannot be appealed at the point of signature. The Act classes this as an "*urgent application*" where a delay would be prejudicial to the person subject to the application.[35]

Form MH06A

Removal order granted by a justice of the peace[36]

This is granted by a justice of the peace and has the same authority as a section 293 warrant. It is not appealable at the point of signature.

Form MH07

Application form to recall (cancel) or vary a removal order[37]
This can be done by anyone claiming to have an interest in the person's welfare. They are applying to have the order recalled or varied to another address. This applies to removal orders signed by either a sheriff or a justice of the peace.

Form MH07A

Form of intimation of hearing of application for recall or variation of removal order under section 295
The Sheriff Clerk sends this out to the person(s) appealing the removal order. It will state the place/date/time of the appeal.

Form MH07B

Order for the recall or variation of a removal order [section 295]
The sheriff would sign this after hearing the appeal from the person subject to the removal order (or his/her representative) or any interested party. This allows the sheriff to either –

- i) recall (that is, cancel) the removal order;[38]
- ii) make an order for the person to be returned to his or her own address or a different address of the person's choice;[39]
- iii) vary the removal order by transferring the person to a different place of safety.[40] The duration of this transfer would be within the 7-day period of the original removal order.

These three conditions have to be completed within 72 hours of the sheriff signing the order.

Note: There are no appeal rights attached to sections 293 or section 295[41]

4) Warrants/orders in general

Practice points

- It may be good practice to take a typed application to the court the day before the hearing. This will allow the sheriff clerk to complete the information necessary for the sheriff to sign the warrant/order if he decides to grant it.
- The order application forms leave space for free text to allow the MHO to give evidence to support the application. This could also be done in a separate sheet depending on the amount of information.
- The section 293 order has no formal heading in Form MHO 5 for the persons accompanying the MHO. This should be referenced as free text to allow them to be recorded in the signed Form MHO5B. The sheriff could miss out the names of the specified person if their names are not available.
- The MHO should specify the number of days required to keep a person in a place of safety. The Act states "*not exceeding 7 days.*"[42]
- The sheriff is likely to ask what will be the care/assessment arrangements during the order period. This would have to be full-time care and may require financial negotiation with social work managers.
- The MHO would normally appear in private alone before the sheriff without witnesses. The MHO should have their named witnesses on standby. The sheriff can then decide after reading the application if he wants to hear any witnesses. The MHO does not need to have named police constables. The MHO can discuss with the police, after obtaining the order, how many officers are required to implement the order. The job of the police is to open lockfast premises, where applicable, and escort the subject of the order to a place of safety.

5) Example of a section 35 Enter Premises warrant (anonymous)

Mental Health (Care and Treatment)(Scotland) Act 2003

Abbreviations for each role:

1. A. = subject of warrant (female)
2. Dr B. = Consultant Psychiatrist
3. Dr C. = General Practitioner
4. Sergeant D. = police constable
5. E. = Local authority council
6. MHO = Mental Health Officer

Information to support the warrant applications to:

1. enter premises under section 35(2)
2. medical examination under section 35(4)

Subject of warrant: A., born [supply full name/insert date of birth].

Warrant address: [insert full postal address].

Applicant: MHO name and workplace address/telephone.

Specified Person: Dr B. Consultant Psychiatrist, hospital address.

Police assistance: Any constable of [insert police force name] (as provided for in section 293(3)(a)(iii) of the 2003 Act).

Period to enact warrant: Up to 8 days from day warrant is signed.

Legal test: Section 33(2) – appearance of

i) mental disorder;
ii) neglect to self;
iii) property suffering damage;
iv) living alone or without care;
v) unable to look after herself or property.

Source of evidence:

1. Dr B. Consultant Psychiatrist

Evidence:

- Dr B. visited A. at home with MHO on [supply date]. A. was verbally threatening and told Dr B. to leave. Dr B. assessed A. as probably having a mental illness of some sort, judging by the neglected state of the house and her dirty appearance. Dr B. quickly withdrew from the doorstep as she felt A. would probably physically threaten her.
- Dr B. anxious to assess A. at home with a view to a hospital admission using civil compulsory powers under the Mental Health (Care and Treatment) (Scotland) Act 2003. The main issue was the safety of the public.

2. Dr C., General Practitioner, [supply surgery address]

Evidence:

- Dr C. referred A. to Dr B. Psychiatry team on [supply date]. His concerns were that A. was shouting at members of the public and physically abusive to some people she knows.
- I spoke to Dr C. on date X and he gave me the following information:

  i) A. has only been seen twice by his practice – specify dates/ illness.
  ii) There was a psychiatric referral made to H. hospital in 19XX where she had been diagnosed with schizoid-type problems. A. did not co-operate with outpatient treatment and was discharged.
  iii) Neighbours reported to his surgery on [specify dates] expressing concern about her behaviour, that is, going out to the street early in the morning. The Health Visitor went three times but could not gain access. A. was annoyed that Health Visitor had called and she denied having any problems.

- I telephoned Sergeant D. on [specify date] as there was another complaint about A.'s behaviour where she had spat on a pedestrian's face and then punched his stomach. This was reported to the police although no charges were pressed.
- On [specify date] Sergeant B. and I discussed this and decided in view of A.'s presentation and recent visit by Dr B., it would be best to seek a warrant to have A. medically examined.

In sum, there is sufficient evidence for a warrant to be used to allow Dr B. to complete a mental health examination. Dr B. has already said she will admit A. to her ward under a short-term detention certificate under section 44 of the 2003 Act if this is appropriate.

6) Example of a section 293 removal order (anonymous)

Abbreviations for each role:

A. = subject of removal order
B. = local authority council
C. = Care Provider
D. = Housing Association
E. = Biological mother
F. = partner of E.
G. = social worker
H. = Manager of Care Provider
Z. = Police Force
MHO = Mental Health Officer (applicant)

FORM MH05

Form of application for removal order under section 293(1)

APPLICATION FOR REMOVAL ORDER UNDER SECTION 293(1) OF THE MENTAL HEALTH (CARE AND TREATMENT) (SCOTLAND) ACT 2003

SHERIFFDOM OF [insert details]

AT [insert name of town court]

I, [insert MHO's name]

being a relevant MHO appointed by B. having its principal offices at [specify address]

hereby apply for a warrant to enter premises at [specify address]

and to remove A., [include full name/insert date of birth]

to the following place of safety

[specify full postal address, normally a hospital]

on the following grounds:–

1. A. was born on [specify]. From an early age A. was accommodated by B. and its statutory predecessor. A Parental Responsibilities Order had been granted in favour of the local authority. A. has no legal relatives.
2. A. currently resides in his own tenancy at [specify address]. He is in receipt of a care package provided by C., an agency that specialises in support for mentally ill people.
3. A. has learning difficulties and suffers from mental illness. A. takes Clozapine, an anti-psychotic drug, which requires regular monitoring with blood tests. A. is presently refusing to undergo such tests. This is a clear example of neglect, which in the long term could severely affect A.'s health. A. requires prompting to take his medication.
4. Approximately six months ago A. secured his current tenancy with D. At that point A.'s biological mother, [E.], appeared in his life together with her partner F.
   E. and F. both appear to abuse alcohol. A.'s social worker G. reports that it appeared that E. and F. might have exploited A. to some extent.
5. E. has now left her home. It is believed that E. is in fear of F.
6. Since E. left, F. spends most of his time in A.'s home, eating and drinking alcohol. F. is verbally abusive and aggressive towards C. staff who attend to A. at his tenancy at the arranged times. F. takes food, alcohol, money and other possessions belonging to A. This frustrates the care plan as A. cannot be left with any money or food as it is liable to be taken by F. It had been intended to introduce A. to elements of independence by assisting him in budgeting and meeting basic needs. However, F.'s exploitation of A. effectively frustrates the care plan.
7. A. has a potential life-threatening heart condition that requires regular monitoring by his general practitioner. There are occasions

when F.'s influence causes A. to refuse to attend with his doctor for such testing. F. is aware of A.'s condition and has been informed of the adverse effect played by alcohol. F. regularly encourages A. to drink to excess and is believed to provide alcohol to A.

8. A. previously stayed in a supported accommodation unit staffed by C. in x village however this unit closed approximately 18 months ago. A. was transferred to another unit. However A. requested to be placed on a waiting list for another supported accommodation unit in another town, which is also staffed by C. In the past 18 months A. has frequently visited this unit and has participated in activities run by C. A place in this Unit has now become available. However, F. has persuaded A. not to take up the place. F. is also preventing A. from contact with G., his allocated social worker.

9. The effect of F.'s presence and influence is significant. A.'s physical and mental health is deteriorating. The neglect and deficiency in care is due to F. preventing C. staff and other agencies from properly administering the care and support package to A.

   A. has reported and protested about F.'s behaviour to C. staff, however it appears that A. is powerless to ask F. to leave his home or stop F. from exploiting him.

10. The purpose of this application is to seek a removal order under section 293 of the 2003 Act in order to remove A. to C.'s accommodation unit as a place of safety. This will remove A. from F.'s extensive exploitation and influence. It is considered that A. is likely to suffer significant harm if not removed to a place of safety.

11. It is further sought that the removal order will authorise the applicant to remove A. to a place of safety along with the specified persons as follows:

    (a) G., Social Worker, B. Council; and
    (b) H., Manager, of C. Provider and
    (c) any constable of Z. (as provided for in section 293(3)(a)(iii) of the 2003 Act).

    G. and H. are both well-known to A.

~~(1) I crave the court to intimate the application to the following persons:~~

~~(a)~~

~~(b) the persons listed below (*being persons prescribed by regulations under section 293(6) of the 2003 Act*):~~

~~Name~~	~~Relationship (*to the person who is the subject of the application*)~~	~~Address~~
~~Indicate if details not known~~		______
~~1.~~	~~nearest relative~~	______
~~2.~~	~~guardian~~	______
~~3.~~	~~welfare attorney~~	______
~~4.~~	~~primary carer~~	______

~~or~~

(2) I crave the court to dispense with intimation on the grounds that delay in obtaining a removal order is likely to be prejudicial to the person, for the following reasons:

1. It is anticipated that F. will become aware of this application for a warrant should it be intimated upon A; and
2. It is considered to be extremely likely that F. will seek to further exploit A. by way of any opportunity which may arise from this application being made; and
3. It is also considered to be reasonably foreseeable that F. may encourage and assist A. in absconding upon the intimation of this application.
4. Accordingly dispensation of intimation under section 393(7) is considered necessary in the circumstances and is sought on the grounds that a delay in obtaining a removal order is likely to be prejudicial to A.

(*Signed*)
Applicant: MHO. Address: [specify full postal address].
Date: specify

Footnotes:

1 section 292 (3)(b) – entry to premises warrant.
2 section 293 – removal order.
3 section 293 for the sheriff; section 294 for a justice of the peace.
4 section 295(1). This applies to a removal order warrant granted by a justice or a sheriff.
5 section 35(9)(b) and section 294. Justices can only operate within their commission area.
6 Note: the Act uses the term "person" in both the inquiry and removal warrants regardless of whether or not they have a mental disorder. The term "patient" only applies where they are subject to compulsory powers.
7 Note: The duty to inquire by a local authority using section 33 is not exclusive to the MHO role.
8 section 33 (1) & (2).
9 section 33(2)(b).
10 section 33(2)(c).
11 section 33(2)(d).
12 section 34.
13 Currently based in Edinburgh.
14 Currently based in Falkirk.
15 Headquarters in Dundee but they have branch offices across Scotland.
16 section 35(11) – note. There is also no appeal if the warrant is refused.
17 section 300.
18 section 35(10).
19 section 293(1) & (2).
20 section 293(2)(b).
21 section 293(2)(c).
22 section 293(1)(c).
23 section 33(1).
24 section 293(3)(a).
25 section 293(3)(c)(ii). The sheriff will expect the MHO to specify the amount of days required in the place of safety. This can be up to 7 days.
26 section 293(5).
27 defined under Scottish Statutory Regulations 2005 No. 381.
28 section 295.
29 section 293(7).
30 section 295(1)(b).
31 section 295(6).
32 CoP, vol 1, chapter 15, para 43, p. 215.
33 CoP, op cit. para 44 & 45, p. 216.
34 see Mental Welfare Commission for Scotland to access the warrant forms online.
35 section 294(b).
36 section 294.
37 section 295(1).
38 section 295(1)(a).
39 section 295(6)(a) or (b).
40 section 295(1)(b)(i).
41 section 296.
42 section 293(3)(c)(ii).

Endnotes:

(A) Section 292(5). The authorised person is any professional involved in the detained patient's care and treatment. This would normally be a nurse or the patient's RMO. In a non-compliance situation, the patient's RMO has discretion over whom he chooses to take a patient into custody (section 113(4)). Where the patient absconds, an MHO may be involved in taking them into custody (section 303(2)).

(B) From 1 December 2007, the two roles of bench and signing justices of the peace are obsolete. These roles are now replaced by the one justice who sits as a justice of the peace in the District Court. The MHO should therefore check with the Clerk of Court for the District Court for a justice to sign warrants. The police should have justice contacts out of hours.

(C) The Criminal Proceedings, etc. (Reform) (Scotland) Act 2007, section 64, plan to abolish District Courts, established in 1975, in favour of justice of the peace Courts (section 59). They will continue to be assisted by a legally-trained clerk (section 63(3)). Effectively the Scottish Courts Service will take over administration of District Courts. The court unification programme should be complete by 2009. This Act received Royal Assent on 18 January 2007.

(D) Section 59(1) AWI 2000 Act. This could include a Council Officer delegated by the Chief Social Work Officer under section 64(9) of the 2000 Act. Note too the powers of the guardian under section 64(1) of the 2000 Act should be relevant to the reasons for the removal order, that is, welfare/finance/property powers, otherwise their right to appeal would be invalid.

(E) Section 16(3)(b) of the 2000 Act. The specific welfare attorney powers have to be relevant to the evidence presented by the MHO in the removal order otherwise the welfare attorney's right to appeal would be invalid.

(F) Section 329(1) page 242, of the Act, under "interpretations". The Act uses the term "individual" to describe a primary carer, thus implying a personal relationship. This therefore excludes a carer in paid employment or a volunteer working for a voluntary organisation, given they can allocate anyone at any time.

(G) Section 294. This should be used sparingly, if at all, as a removal order would usually be planned in advance given the MHO has to specify the place of safety. If the person needs to be removed urgently, say, to a hospital, the MHO may wish to use a section 35(1) warrant with a medical practitioner who can then complete a civil compulsory certificate. Access then to a sheriff or justice is equally acceptable as there are no follow-up appeal rights. (section 35(11)).

Chapter 7

Named Person

1) Introduction

The main purpose of this chapter is to detail the responsibility an MHO has in identifying and assessing the appropriateness of a named person; then carrying out a range of legal notification duties as described in previous chapters.

Summary points:

- The concept of a named person in the Act is unique in that it cannot be transferred from any other legislation, notably Adults with Incapacity (Scotland) Act 2000. This means people appointed as attorneys or welfare guardians have no automatic right to be named persons.
- The named person role is extensive. They can act independently from the detained patient and must also be consulted and notified in different procedures as described in previous chapters.
- Only individuals can be a named person. This does not include employees of any health or care services unless they choose to act as individuals. If so, there may be a conflict of interest with their employers.
- The nominator can withdraw a nomination if they complete a withdrawal form witnessed by a prescribed witness.
- The nominator can also declare whom they do not want to act as named persons through a form witnessed by a prescribed person. The Tribunal can, however, ignore this declaration. The named person can decline their nomination by writing to the nominator and the local authority where the nominator lives.

2) Information points

- The MHO has sole legal responsibility to establish whether a detained patient has a named person, for example, "*take such steps as are reasonably practicable.*"[1]
- There are two legal routes for a patient having a named person:

i) Nomination under section 250

- Any person living in Scotland who is over 16 years of age can nominate a named person. The named person must be over 16 years of age and ordinarily resident in the United Kingdom, the Channel Islands or the Isle of Man.[2]
- A nomination can only be legal if witnessed by a prescribed person who verifies the person nominating understands the effect of the nomination and has not been subjected to any undue influence in making the nomination.[3]
- The prescribed persons are listed in regulations as follows:[4]

  a) clinical psychologists entered on the British Psychological Society's register of chartered psychologists;
  b) medical practitioners;
  c) occupational therapists registered with the Health Professions Council;
  d) persons employed in the provision of (or in managing the provision of) a care service;
  e) registered nurses;
  f) social workers; and
  g) solicitors.

ii) Default appointment under section 251

- This is when no person is nominated or a nominated person declines to act. The potential nominator may be a detained patient with poor capacity or no capacity to make a formal nomination. The MHO must check this out with the patient's RMO rather than assume blanket incapacity.

- The order of appointment for a default named person would be:

  a) patient's primary carer – that is, the person caring for the patient immediately before the detention, for example, relative/partner/friend/neighbour.[5]

  b) patient's nearest relative. This would apply if the patient were living alone with no primary carer. The blood status hierarchy of nearest relative is listed under section 254(2).

MHO role in a) & b) above

- They are basically the same thing, that is, to establish whether or not the nominated or default named person is prepared to carry out the named person role.
- The Code of Practice gives practical guidance to the MHO to ensure that the nominated/default named person knows what they are taking on and also to be given the chance to opt out of that role. This is described in the Code as *"best practice"*.[6]
- The MHO has an inspectorial role to assess the suitability or otherwise of either a nominated or a default named person. This could include abusive situations such as parents or carers. Moreover, where the MHO has a specific duty to identify a named person, for example, before consenting to a short-term detention certificate[7] or applying for a CTO[8], the MHO has a mandatory duty to apply to the Tribunal for an order under section 257 removing that *"acting named person"* and where appropriate, the Tribunal may grant a replacement.[9]
- The MHO has only discretionary powers to apply to the Tribunal under section 257 if they come across a situation where a person has no named person or if that named person is inappropriate, that is, in section 257(7) – where the word *"may"* is printed.
- This general right to apply to the Tribunal to have a named person replaced extends to the patient, patient's RMO, if the patient is a child, anyone with parental responsibilities, hospital managers, any welfare attorney/guardian/relative of the patient, or any other person having an interest in the welfare of the patient.[10]
- This application under section 256 could have interesting possibilities, for example, where the patient is under 16 years of age, say, against

a parent; a divorced parent can also object to the nomination of their former spouse as named person; an adult patient who has been unable to revoke or nominate a named person because a prescribed witness does not certify capacity.[11]

- The Code of Practice advises it would be good practice for the MHO "*to ensure the named person's identity is made known to all those who have a direct interest and at least to the patient's RMO, carer, independent advocate and legal representative.*[12]
- The Act requires the MHO to notify the AMP of the named person before giving consent to a short-term detention certificate. If the MHO cannot establish a named person they have to write to the AMP notifying them of the steps taken to comply with that duty. This has to be done within 7 days of being consulted by the AMP. This addresses the issue of night work or, say, the MHO being on duty and not having the full information at hand.[13]

3) Administration: notifications (Letters 1-6)

To facilitate this process – regardless of whether a named person is nominated or appointed by default – the following are suggested standard letters (in order of logic) – see Chapter 9 for templates:

Letter 1

◆ **MHO to named person confirming their agreement to be either a nominated/default named person.**

There is also a sentence which states the following:

> *"Should you not wish to formally act as a named person please sign and return the attached letter, addressed to myself."*

Letter 2

◆ Named person to MHO declining the nomination.

- Named person [nominated or default] declines the nomination.
- Legal reference:
  - a) section 251(5) page 176 – primary carer declines.
  - b) section 254(5) page 178 – nearest relative declines.
- The named person has to send a copy of this letter to the local authority and also to the person subject to the application. The solution may be for the named person to write to the MHO who can then send a copy to that person.
- The MHO may want to include a pre-paid envelope given they only have 7 days to take the steps of establishing a named person.
- If the named person verbally declines nomination and refuses to put this in writing, the MHO should record this as a substitute

Letter 3

◆ MHO to patient's RMO confirming the patient's named person.

Letter 4

◆ MHO to Tribunal/Commission regarding steps taken to establish a named person and also reasons why MHO did not nominate an alternative named person.[14]

Suggested reasons could be:

- a) it is best to wait until the patient recovers capacity to allow them to make that nomination; or
- b) the MHO has no nominations to make.

- The MHO has to establish whether the patient has a named person. If there is a named person [nominated/default], then they shall be the named person. If the MHO however considers this named person – called the *"apparent named person"* in section 255(7)(b) is inappropriate, the MHO must apply to the Tribunal under section 257 giving their reasons for this inappropriateness.

- The Tribunal may then make an order declaring that this *"apparent named person"* is no longer the named person. The Tribunal has discretion to have that named person replaced although that would only happen if the MHO submitted another nomination.[15]

Letter 5

◆ **MHO to Tribunal regarding inappropriateness of an apparent named person.**[16]

There is no guidance of what "inappropriate" means. The Code of Practice[17] states:

> *"In this respect, the MHO is under a duty to assess the appropriateness of the named person for that role. The expectation is that the patient's right to choose whom they wish to have as a named person would be respected. Proposals to override those wishes should only be made where there are clear and significant reasons for doing so"*

Note: *"clear and significant reasons"* could include abusive parents in the case of a child; exploitative relatives for adults. It would be the duty of other professionals to raise these issues for the MHO to make such an application.

Letter 6

◆ **Named person [nominated or default] writes to the Tribunal requesting no notification and also to waive their consultation rights for changes in the proposed measures or granting an interim CTO.**

- The named person may not wish to be involved in the Tribunal, that is, to receive notification or any documents. They still, however, remain the named person.
- Furthermore if the Tribunal chooses to grant additional measures other than the ones proposed by the MHO or to grant an interim CTO,

they have a legal requirement to consult the named person for their views before granting the measures or an interim CTO.

- It would be useful, therefore, to include these possibilities in a letter from the named person to the Tribunal, which would then avoid legal problems.[18]

Footnotes:

1 section 255(2).
2 section 254(6).
3 section 250(2)(b).
4 Scottish Statutory Instrument 2004 No. 430. The Mental Health (Patient Representation) (Prescribed Persons) (Scotland) (No. 2) Regulations 2004.
5 section 251(1).
6 CoP, vol.1. chapter 6, para 33, p. 91.
7 section 45(1)(b).
8 section 59.
9 section 255(6), where the word "shall" is printed.
10 section 256(2).
11 I am grateful to Franks, R A & Cobb, D (2005) op cit, General Note, p. 288 for pointing this out.
12 CoP, vol. 1; chapter 6; para 34, p. 91.
13 section 45(3)(b); section 59. The review forms from August 2007 however adapt this situation.
14 section 255(5).
15 section 255(6).
16 section 255(6).
17 CoP, vol 1, chapter 6; para 41, p. 93.
18 section 64(7).

Chapter 8

Social Circumstances Reports

Content

The Act requires the MHO to complete an SCR within 21 days of a *"relevant event"* occurring. These are listed in section 232 as follows: Note: s, = section; ss. = subsection

- the granting of a short-term detention certificate [s. 44];
- the making of the following orders/directions:
  - an interim compulsory treatment order [s. 65];
  - a compulsory treatment order [s. 64(a)];
  - an assessment order [s. 130 ss. 52D];
  - a treatment order [s. 130 ss.52M];
  - an interim compulsion order [s. 131 ss. 53(2); p. 95];
  - a compulsion order [s. 133 ss. 57A; p.100];
  - a hospital direction; or [s. 59A of 1995 Act; p. 45];[1]
  - a transfer for treatment direction [s.136(2); p. 108].

The Mental Health (social circumstances reports)(Scotland) Regulations 2005 No. 310 give listed guidelines on the information to include in an SCR. The list is made up of nineteen headings that lends itself to an easier style of recording. The regulation qualifies using this list *"where it is relevant to the care of the patient"*. [2] The headings are as follows:

1. the reasons for the use of compulsory powers;
2. the views of the patient with respect to the use of compulsory powers;
3. if the patient is unable to give a view, and only if available to the MHO, the views of the patient's named person, carer, guardian and welfare attorney with respect to the use of compulsory powers;
4. the patient's state of mental health;
5. the patient's state of physical health;

6. the patient's mental health history;
7. an assessment of the risk of harm to the patient and to others;
8. the patient's personal history including details of employment, finances and accommodation prior to the use of compulsory powers;
9. details of the patient's family situation including whether the patient has children, dependents and caring responsibilities;
10. details of the patient's regular social contacts;
11. the patient's ability to care for himself or herself;
12. the care being provided to the patient prior to the use of compulsory powers;
13. any matters which would require the local authority to make inquiries into the patient's case under section 33 of the Mental Health (Care and Treatment) (Scotland) Act 2003;
14. any alternatives to the use of compulsory powers which were considered and ruled out;
15. any history of offending, including consideration of victims and those affected;
16. any history of substance misuse;
17. ethnic, cultural and religious factors;
18. whether the patient has difficulty in communicating; and
19. any plan which has been put in place to deal with any of the above.

- The purpose of the reports is to assist the patient's responsible medical officer (RMO) and the Mental Welfare Commission for Scotland to fulfil their functions. This would help the RMO, for example, to decide on the merits of a further order.
- There is no requirement for a copy of the report to be provided to the patient, the patient's named person or any other person. Indeed this should be discouraged, as the patient will have access to the MHO's account of their personal circumstances within the context of a CTO application.
- The Act allows the MHO discretion as to whether or not to prepare an SCR. The legal guideline is the SCR "*would serve little, or no, practical purpose*".[3] This could be where an SCR has been completed for a previous relevant event such as a short-term detention certificate and the circumstances have not changed. It could also be where the RMO

has decided not to pursue further detention.

- The MHO should always bear in mind the purpose of an SCR and whether or not it will be used by the RMO. The Commission have already stated they will not routinely read SCRs but instead refer to them when doing their statutory review duties when patients are detained in either a hospital or a community-based CTO.[4]
- The MHO must record the reasons for their view in the space provided in the statutory SCR form and send a copy to the patient's RMO and Mental Welfare Commission.[5] It may be helpful for the MHO to update the patient's circumstances in this section without having to complete a full history.
- The contents of the SCR could be transposed into other reports. This is particularly helpful when the MHO is meeting tight deadlines. A good example is the Form CTO 1 under *"personal circumstances"* [text box 3] The MHO may want to make explicit the source of the information and which of the nineteen headings have been selected. The guidance for this text box includes the term *"relevance"* which allows the MHO flexibility in interpretation.

Sample 1

◆ MHO gives reasons for deciding that an SCR would serve little, or no, practical purpose [section 231(2)(b)(i)]

Reasons: SCR already prepared for a recent relevant event linked to the patients present order.

1. The MHO [insert name] prepared an SCR after the following relevant event as listed under section 232 – short-term detention certificate/an interim compulsory treatment order/compulsory treatment order/assessment order/treatment order/an interim compulsion order/compulsion order/hospital direction/transfer for treatment order [delete where not relevant] on .... [insert date].
2. There have been no changes in the patient's social circumstances since this relevant event took place.
3. Patient's relevant event is due to expire on [insert date].

Sample 2

◆ MHO gives reasons for deciding that an SCR would serve little, or no, practical purpose but includes an update summary from the previous SCR [section 231(2)(b)(i)]

Reasons: SCR has/has not been completed recently but no significant changes in patient's social circumstances. MHO however supplies an update.[6]

1. Patient was placed under the relevant event as recorded for the following reason – to receive electro-convulsive therapy under section 237 of the 2003 Act [example].
2. Dr X. responsible medical officer has stated this treatment should be completed within the current order.
3. An SCR was completed on [insert date] or no SCRs have been completed [delete as appropriate].

The following example is a summary of events leading to patient's admission.

The purpose of this certificate was purely to give the patient ECT treatment for depression.

1. Patient initially admitted to X hospital, on an informal basis from [date]. The treatment was for depression following his partner's death in [date]. Patient's symptoms worsened the week before the current certificate started on [date] to the extent he was not eating/drinking and refusing medication. Patient had originally agreed to ECT treatment due to start on [date] but on the day, he refused to attend. Patient's RMO contacted self as duty MHO for [date] to give consent to a section 44 short-term detention certificate.
2. Patient has had three ECT treatments so far with little obvious effect. Patient's RMO said at the point of detention the process would probably take about two weeks, that is, four ECT treatments. It is, therefore, still too early to gauge progress.

3. Patient's partner died recently on [date] after only two days illness. Patient reacted badly to this bereavement. The medical notes indicate patient complaining of "*fuzziness in head/hearing loss/bowel problems*". Patient has been checked out for these complaints with no obvious symptoms present. The SHO summarised her assessment as follows: "*Introduced idea that he may be focusing on somatic complaints because of mental illness but he appeared to be lacking insight into why he is in hospital.*"
4. Patient was born in [place]; married in [year]; wife came from the same area; one child (son). Patient lives alone but son has been living with patient since wife's death; son very caring and sacrificial in outlook, that is, thinking of giving up his work to look after patient on a permanent basis. Patient's RMO has already advised son not to do this.
5. Self saw patient in ward together with RMO. Patient repeating his opposition to ECT saying it would do no good. His main focus was on bowel problems and lack of sleep that he felt was not being taken seriously.

   Self also present later the same morning when patient's son was speaking to RMO. Patient's son in agreement with the ECT treatment and also the use of a short-term detention certificate to give patient this on a compulsory basis if necessary. Son too in agreement to be patient's default named person under section 251(1) of the 2003 Act.

   In sum, this certificate was appropriate. It is being used solely for the purpose of giving patient ECT therapy to relieve his depressive symptoms. Patient initially willing to receive the treatment but on the day of his first ECT he refused saying he had felt he was being forced to sign the form and had no idea what ECT entailed, that is, the risks and benefits. RMO notes, however, this had been explained several times.

   I gave consent as patient's physical and mental state was deteriorating. I am assured by the RMO that the patient's symptoms will be relieved within two weeks of treatment.

Sample 3

◆ Full SCR using the Regulation guidelines[7] [section 213(3)]

Scottish Statutory Instrument 2005 No. 310 – guidelines. (a)-(s)

Abbreviations used in each role:

1. Patient – the legal term used for the person subject to the report.[8]
2. A. = duty Mental Health Officer.
3. Dr. B = patient's responsible medical officer [RMO].
4. C. – patient's community psychiatric nurse [CPN].
4. x = date.

a) The reasons for the use of compulsory powers

Patient had left the ward where he was an informal patient. Patient went to a local pub and started to drink excessively. Patient's behaviour became aggressive and he was returned to the ward by the Police and later formally detained. See letters from A. who consented to both the emergency and short-term detention certificate, dated x.

b) The views of the patient with respect to the use of compulsory powers

Patient's main objections are the change in medication which Dr. B. prescribed at the point of admission on x. He has refused this medication. It has now been stopped in line with patient's wishes and patient to commence on different medication.

c) If the patient is unable to give a view, and only if available to the Mental Health Officer, the views of the patient's named person, carer, guardian and welfare attorney with respect to the use of compulsory powers

I tried unsuccessfully several times to contact the patient's default named person (son). I sent him a letter explaining the role and gave him the chance of withdrawing from this (default) role. A. did contact the named person at the point of giving consent. His view was that the patient should stop drinking which would help his mental health. Named person has been in telephone contact with patient.

d) The patient's state of mental health

Patient's mental health has improved. Patient has a bi-polar mental disorder and has been responding well to treatment.

e) The patient's state of physical health

Patient enjoys good health.

Or: Patient has the following major physical illness [list]. They are being treated in the ward with patient's consent or patient unable to give consent so a section 47 certificate under the Adult's with Incapacity (Scotland) Act 2000 has been issued by patient's RMO.

f) The patient's mental health history

Patient was diagnosed as having a mental disorder in [year]. Patient has had four formal admissions since then dating back to [year]. The admissions have always been for short periods and then a discharge home with an informal agreement to keep outpatient appointments with his psychiatrist.

g) An assessment of the risk of harm to the patient and to others [9]

Patient can be verbally aggressive in the ward but only when he has returned to the ward as an informal patient in an inebriate state.

h) The patient's personal history including details of employment, finances and accommodation prior to the use of compulsory powers

These matters are detailed in previous SCRs dated x.[10] Patient gets full state benefits as a result of his mental illness. He chooses to spend some of it regularly on alcohol and drugs.

i) Details of the patient's family situation including whether the patient has children, dependents and caring responsibilities

Patient is divorced with two sons. The eldest lives abroad, hence why he is not the default named person under section 251(5).[11] The youngest keeps in contact by telephone and the occasional visit.

j) **Details of the patient's regular social contacts**
Patient's main social contact is through his local pub. He also spends a great deal of time at home playing music.

k) **The patient's ability to care for himself or herself**
Patient is able to manage self-care. This also applies to domestic care depending on his mood.

l) **The care being provided to the patient prior to the use of compulsory powers**
Patient lives alone by choice, preferring his own company. Patient does not require personal care or any other form of care services.

m) **Any matters which would require the local authority to make inquiries into the patient's case under section 33 of the Mental Health (Care and Treatment) (Scotland) Act 2003**
Patient volunteered himself to hospital owing to a build up of his bipolar illness which had been deteriorating over the past 6-8 weeks prior to admission when he had started drinking heavily.

n) **Any alternatives to the use of compulsory powers which were considered and ruled out**
Given patient was already an informal patient in the ward where he left and became intoxicated, there was no alternative but to use compulsory civil detention powers as detailed in the MHO letters.

o) **Any history of offending, including consideration of victims and those affected**[12]
None.

p) **Any history of substance misuse**
Patient has used cannabis now for many years. He sees this as part of his lifestyle.

q) Ethnic, cultural and religious factors[13]
Not applicable.

r) Whether the patient has difficulty in communicating
Has no communication difficulties.
Note: if the patient has communication difficulties it is best to explain why that is the case e.g. the patient does not speak English.

s) Any plan which has been put in place to deal with any of the above
Patient enjoys a good relationship with C., his CPN. He also attends the Lithium clinic at the clinic. This plan will resume after discharge. The other issue will be to encourage patient to make an advance statement to deal with issues of medication and patient management should he wish to leave the ward to drink excessively.
Or:
Patient's RMO has requested self to apply for a compulsory treatment order.

Optional summary text:

This certificate was necessary and fulfilled the five legal tests for a short-term detention as follows:

i) section 44(4)(a) – mental disorder.
ii) section 44(4)(b) – significant impairment.
Long history of self-neglect.
iii) section 44(4)(c) – hospital detention necessary to treat.
Home-based care would not work.
iv) section 44(4)(d) – risk to self in terms of health/safety.
Similar argument to section 44(4)(c) above.
v) section 44(4)(e) – necessity. Patient wanting to go home so unlikely to take any care or treatment as an informal patient.

Footnotes:

1 1995 Act refers to the Criminal Procedure (Scotland) Act 1995.

2 The Mental Health (social circumstances reports)(Scotland) Regulations 2005 No. 310. Web site reference under Scottish legislation.

3 section 231(2)(a) and (b).

4 section 51 [power to revoke short-term certificates] & section 98 [power to revoke CTOs]. Both are discretionary powers.

5 section 231(1)(b).

6 The Act allows the MHO to exercise judgement over this issue. The summary update content can therefore vary to support this judgement.

7 This SCR gives information in response to specific questions from each heading as opposed to a summary update in Sample 2. The MHO may wish to expand these points where relevant. It should be borne in mind however the information will only be used by the patient's RMO to assist them in deciding on further powers. The Commission will only refer to the SCR where they have statutory visiting duties or for appeal purposes (unlikely). An SCR should be a summary of shared discussion and agreements between the MHO and RMO, not a substitute.

8 Given this is an anonymous example, I have used the term "patient" throughout the report instead of a full name.

9 This could be expanded according to the level of risk patient put themselves or others either before or during detention. The care plan notes in patient's medical file should give details.

10 The MHO has discretion whether or not to quote the contents of a previous SCR. Both the Commission and the patient's RMO should have this on file.

11 Note: The Act states the default named person (in this case the youngest son as nearest relative) has to be ordinarily resident in the United Kingdom, the Channel Islands or the Isle of Man. [section254(6)(c)]. If the patient was ordinarily resident abroad, for example, a visitor from Australia taken ill, the nearest relative could be anywhere worldwide. The primary carer status would not change, as this would be the person who was giving the patient substantial unpaid care before admission. Circumstances would dictate this issue.

12 This would be more relevant for criminal proceedings reports although the author is not sure how victim's views would be obtained.

13 An obvious example would be where interpreters were used before detaining a patient.

Chapter 9

MHO Notifications – suggested template letters

1) Chapter 2: Emergency[1]/short-term detention certificates

Summary of letters:

Ⓐ **Letter 1**	MHO to medical practitioner (GP; SHO; AMP) confirming consent/non-consent of emergency/short-term detention certificate.
Ⓑ **Letter 2**	MHO to named person reference appeal/advocacy rights for a short-term detention certificate.
Ⓒ **Letter 3**	MHO to patient reference appeal/advocacy rights for a short-term detention certificate.
Ⓓ **Letter 4**	MHO to Independent Advocacy Services informing them of the section 44 certificate.

Ⓐ Letter 1: MHO to medical practitioner (GP; SHO; AMP) confirming consent/non-consent of emergency/short-term detention certificate[2]

To: .... Medical Practitioner

Address: ....

Date: ....

Dear Dr ....

Subject: .... d.o.b. ....

Community Health Index Number: ....

Social Work reference: ....

Home Address: ....

Statute/Date/expiry of certificate (where relevant) ....

This is to inform you I did/did not give consent to the above statute for reasons as follows: (freetext)

....

Yours sincerely

....

MHO

Ⓑ Letter 2: MHO to named person reference appeal/advocacy rights for a short-term detention certificate

To .... named person

From: .... Mental Health Officer

Named person's address: ....

Date: ....

Dear Mr/Mrs/Ms ....

Re. Detention of .... under Section .... of the Mental Health (Care and Treatment) (Scotland) Act 2003 (the "2003 Act")

Date/expiry of certificate order (where relevant): ....

Hospital: ....

Psychiatrist/responsible medical officer: ....

I understand the above patient has nominated you as their named person **<u>or</u>** you automatically became the named person by default as the primary carer or nearest relative under Section 251 of the 2003 Act (delete which does not apply).

As named person you have the following rights in relation to the above patient:

1. You will receive written information by the hospital managers about the detention certificate and in more detail about your responsibilities as a named person.
2. You will have an independent right of appeal against the detention order to the Mental Health Tribunal for Scotland, based in Hamilton. You will be entitled to free Legal Aid.
3. The Psychiatrist will consult you if there are any proposed changes to the care plan.

Should you **not** wish to formally act as a named person please sign and return the attached form, addressed to myself.

The following is my understanding of your wishes so far (where relevant)

Freetext: ....

Yours sincerely

....
MHO/Designated MHO

cc RMO, Patient, Health Records, X Hospital and others (where appropriate)

Ⓒ Letter 3: MHO to patient reference appeal/advocacy rights for a short-term detention certificate

To: . . . . Patient

Address: . . . . Patient's current address

Date: ....

Dear Mr/Mrs/Ms ....

Subject: . . . .

Date/expiry of short-term certificate order (where relevant) . . . .

Further to your detention I am legally obliged under section 45(1) of the Mental Health (Care and Treatment) (Scotland) Act 2003 (the "2003 Act") to inform you of the following:

1. You have been placed on a .... detention certificate which started on .... and ends on .... [28 days].
2. Your Psychiatrist can stop this certificate at any time within the 28-period if they think you no longer need formal detention. You can then choose to remain in hospital on a voluntary basis or discharge yourself, with or without medical agreement.
3. You have a right of appeal against this short-term certificate to the Mental Health Tribunal for Scotland, Hamilton under Section 50(1) of the 2003 Act. You will be entitled to free Legal Aid.
4. You have the right of an independent advocacy services under Section 259 of the 2003 Act. I have contacted them about your detention. They will make contact in due course.

The following is my understanding of your wishes so far.

Freetext: . . . .

Yours sincerely

....
MHO/Designated MHO

Witnessed by: (optional) ....

Profession: ....

Date: ....

Ⓓ Letter 4: MHO to independent advocacy services informing them of the section 44 certificate

....

Independent Advocacy Worker
Office address:

Date: ....

Dear ....

Re: Notification under section 45(1)(d) of the Mental Health (Care and Treatment) (Scotland) Act 2003 [" 2003 Act"]

Statute: section 44 of the 2003 Act. Short-term detention certificate

Subject of application/Community Index Number (where known):

....

....

Subject's current address:

....

Current statute (where applicable)..

I am obliged under section 45(1)(d) of the 2003 Act to take appropriate steps to ensure that the patient has the opportunity of making use of your services. I have informed the above person that your service is available for use under section 259 of the 2003 Act.

Freetext: . . . .

Yours faithfully

....

MHO/Designated MHO

2) Chapter 3: Compulsory treatment order application

Summary of letters:

Ⓐ Letter 1 MHO to patient informing them of their rights/availability of advocacy services/informing the patient that the application is being made [Section 61(1)(a)-(d)].

Ⓑ Letter 2 MHO to named person informing them of the CTO application [Section 60(1)(b)].

Ⓒ Letter 3 MHO letter to the Mental Welfare Commission reference CTO application under section 60(1)(c).

Ⓓ Letter 4 MHO to independent advocacy services about the CTO application [Section 61(2)(d)(ii)].

Ⓐ Letter 1: MHO to patient re: informing of rights/availability of advocacy services/inform patient the application is being made [section 61(1)(a)-(d)]

To: .... Patient

Address: ....

Date: ....

Subject: ....

I am legally obliged under section 60(1)(b) of the Mental Health (Care and Treatment) (Scotland) Act 2003 (the "2003 Act") to inform you of the following:

1. Dr. ...., your Psychiatrist, has requested I apply to the Mental Health Tribunal for Scotland for a compulsory treatment order. This means you may be placed either in hospital or in the community, initially for up to six months. Your Psychiatrist can stop this at any time within this period.

2. You have a legal right to oppose this application at the tribunal hearing. If you choose a solicitor to represent you, then you will be entitled to free Legal Aid. The Tribunal will send you a letter advising you where and when the hearing is to take place. You will also receive a copy of the application form prepared by myself and also two mental health reports prepared by your Psychiatrist and a General Practitioner or another Psychiatrist.

3. You have the right to use independent advocacy services under Section 259 of the 2003 Act. The contact address/telephone number is: ....

If you are already in hospital, a ward nurse can contact them on your behalf.

It is also part of my duty under section 61(2) (d) of the 2003 Act to make this process as easy as possible. To this end, I have informed the independent Advocacy Service who will make contact with you. [see free text below for more personal details regarding yourself].

I am also legally obliged under section 60(1)(b) and section 60(1)(c) of the 2003 Act to inform your named person, if you have one, and also the Mental Welfare Commission respectively, of this application. Your named person can also oppose this compulsory treatment order application and have free legal aid should they wish to have a solicitor to represent them.

Your named person is:..

This person was nominated by yourself under section 250 OR is a default named person under section 251. [delete as appropriate]

The following information is my understanding of your wishes so far.

Freetext: . . . .

Yours sincerely

....
MHO/Designated MHO

Ⓑ Letter 2. MHO to named person informing them of the CTO application [section 60(1)(b)]

To: .... named person

Address: ....

Date: ....

Subject: ....

I am legally obliged under section 60(1)(b) of the Mental Health (Care and Treatment)(Scotland) Act 2003 (the "2003 Act") to inform you of the following in relation to

.................................., hereafter termed "Subject".

You will be acting in the role of nominated/default named person under section 250/251/252 of the 2003 Act. [delete where not appropriate]

1. Dr. ...., Subject's Psychiatrist, has requested I apply to the Mental Health Tribunal for Scotland for a compulsory treatment order. This means the Subject may be placed either in hospital or in the community, initially for up to six months. The Psychiatrist can stop this order at any time within this period when they think the Subject can either remain in hospital on a voluntary basis for further treatment or be discharged.

2. You have a legal right to oppose this application at the tribunal hearing. If you need a solicitor to represent you, you will be entitled to free Legal Aid. The Tribunal will send you a letter when and where the hearing is to take place. You will also receive from them a copy of the application form prepared by myself along with two mental health reports prepared by the Subject's Psychiatrist and a General Practitioner or another Psychiatrist.

The following information is my understanding of your wishes so far.

Freetext: ....

Yours sincerely

....

MHO/Designated MHO

⊙ Letter 3: MHO letter to the Mental Welfare Commission reference CTO application under section 60(1)(c)

Mental Welfare Commission
K. Floor
Argyll House
3 Lady Lawson Street
EDINBURGH
EH3 9FH

Date: ....

Dear Sir/Madam,

Re: Notification under section 60(1)(c) of the Mental Health (Care and Treatment) (Scotland) Act 2003

Subject of application/Community Health Index Number (where known):

. . . .

. . . .

Subject's current address: [home/hospital]

. . . .

Current certificate/expiry date: . . . .

I am obliged under section 60(1)(c) of the Mental Health (Care and Treatment) (Scotland) Act 2003 to inform you that Dr. ...., responsible medical officer for the above person, has asked me to make an application to the Mental Health Tribunal for Scotland for a compulsory treatment order.

Yours faithfully

....
MHO/Designated MHO

Ⓓ Letter 4. MHO to independent advocacy services about the CTO application [section 61(2)(d)(ii)]

....
Advocacy Worker
Office address:

Dear ....

Re: Notification under section 61(2)(d) of the Mental Health (Care and Treatment) (Scotland) Act 2003 ["the 2003 Act"]

Application: section 63 of the 2003 Act. Compulsory treatment order

Subject of application/Community Index Number (where known):

. . . .

. . . .

Subject's current address:

. . . .

Current statute/expiry (where applicable) . . . .

I am obliged under section 61(2)(c)(ii) of the 2003 Act to inform the above person that your service is available for use under section 259 of the 2003 Act.

Freetext: . . . .

Yours faithfully

....
MHO/Designated MHO

3) Chapter 4: CTO Reviews. Stage C – Notification by MHO

There are three letters that cover the statutory notifications as follows:

Ⓐ **Letter 1** MHO to patient and named person informing them of the RMO's proposal; rights of appeal; availability of independent advocacy.

Ⓑ **Letter 2** MHO to RMO reference agreement/disagreement with the proposal – adapted according to the type of review.

Ⓒ **Letter 3** MHO to Independent Advocacy Service reference CTO review.[3]

Ⓐ Letter 1: MHO to patient and named person[4] informing him of the RMO's proposal; rights of appeal; availability of independent advocacy

Dear Mr/Mrs/Ms ....

Subject: ....

Date/expiry of compulsory order (where relevant) ....

Further to your detention I am legally obliged under section 85/89 [delete] of the Mental Health (Care and Treatment) (Scotland) Act 2003 (the "2003 Act") to inform you of the following:

You were placed on a compulsory treatment order/compulsion order [delete] by a tribunal hearing, which started on .... and ends on ....

Dr. .... your Psychiatrist wishes to review this order to include the following [delete where not applicable].

i) Extend the order by another 6 or 12 months. [delete where not applicable]
ii) Vary the order to include the measures listed below. [delete measures where not applicable]
iii) Extend and vary the order to include the measures listed below. [delete measures where not applicable]

Measures available to the Tribunal:

1. section 66(1)(a) – detention in a specified hospital – [name of hospital].
2. section 66(1)(b) – giving of medical treatment under Part 16 of the 2003 Act.
3. section 66(1)(c) – attendance for medical treatment.
4. section 66(1)(d) – attendance to receive community care services.
5. section 66(1)(e) – reside at a specified place – [name of place].
6. section 66(1)(f) - access requirement.
7. section 66(1)(g) – approval of MHO to any proposed change of address.
8. section 66(1)(h) – patient to inform MHO of any change of address.

Dr. .... has to apply to the Mental Health Tribunal for Scotland based in Hamilton, South Lanarkshire to have the measures changed. You and ...., your named person, have a separate legal right to be heard at a tribunal hearing under section 103(5)[5] of the 2003 Act before they make a decision. You and your named person will be entitled to free Legal Aid.

You have the right of an independent advocacy services under Section 259 of the 2003 Act. I have written to this service based in .... , about the application. They will be in contact with you at some point

Or

it is my understanding you do not wish this service. [delete where not applicable]

The following is my understanding of your wishes so far

(freetext) . . . .

Yours sincerely

....
MHO

cc named person

Ⓑ Letter 2: MHO to RMO reference agreement/disagreement with the proposal – adapted according to the type of review

To: .... responsible medical officer

Address: ....

Date: ....

Dear Dr ....

Patient: .... d.o.b. ....

Current address: ....

Community Health Index Number: ....

Hospital reference number: ....

Social work reference number: ....

Review of Civil/Criminal order/date (where relevant) ....

1) section 77(3)(c)(i) – first mandatory review of a compulsory treatment order
2) section 78(3) – further mandatory reviews of a compulsory treatment order
3) section 93[6] – MHO consultation – time to time review to vary a compulsory treatment order.

This is to inform you that I am discharging my duties under number .... above in the Mental Health (Care and Treatment) (Scotland) Act 2003 (the Act), to provide a report in response to your mandatory review consultation.

MHO Duties as follows: [delete where appropriate]

1. section 85(2)(d)
   MHO's duty to inform RMO whether they agree/disagree with extending client's CTO by [insert] months.
2. section 93(4)(c)
   RMO to consult the MHO to vary the CTO.
3. section 89(2)(e)
   MHO's duty to inform RMO whether they agree/disagree with extending and varying the CTO.

Measures to be varied: [delete as appropriate]
1. section 66(1)(a) – detention in a specified hospital – [name of hospital].
2. section 66(1)(b) – giving of medical treatment under Part 16 of the 2003 Act.
3. section 66(1)(c) – attendance for medical treatment.

4. section 66(1)(d) – attendance to receive community care services.
5. section 66(1)(e) – reside at a specified place – [name of place].
6. section 66(1)(f) – access requirement.
7. section 66(1)(g) – approval of MHO to any proposed change of address.
8. section 66(1)(h) – patient to inform MHO of any change of address.

Reasons for agreement/disagreement:

(freetext) ....

Patient continues to meet the criteria for detention for the following reasons:

[freetext] ....

Additional information: (case example given with each heading)

The Tribunal have ancillary powers under section 109(2) of the 2003 Act to request an MHO report where they are not satisfied they have sufficient information to enable them to make a decision on review applications. The content of this report is based on the Mental Health (compulsory treatment orders – documents and reports to be submitted to the Tribunal) (Scotland) Regulations 2005 No.366.

The MHO report states a list of issues to include in this report as follows is required to address the following issues. (Sample included for guidance)

a) the views of the Mental Health Officer on the determination and the reasons for those views.

View: agree/disagree with the determination.

Reasons: As discussed with yourself and Staff Nurse A. on [date] following patient's review in B. Unit, patient still requires compulsory powers given his vulnerable lifestyle and the negative symptoms of his illness. The reasons are recorded in Form CTO3a. Patient still requires medical treatment as defined in section 329.

(b) if known to the Mental Health Officer, the views of the patient and the patient's named person on the determination and the reasons for those views.

Self-interviewed patient on [date]. Patient does not agree with the detention. He saw his solicitor earlier in the afternoon of [date] and intends to appeal the CTO. Patient would like to leave B. Unit and proceed to supported accommodation.

I spoke to C., patient's mother and default named person under section 251(5) of the 2003 Act, on [date]. She is in agreement with the CTO being extended. She would not support her son's appeal but at the same time feels he should be allowed to appeal which will allow him to hear an independent view on the issue of detention from the Tribunal system.

(c) in so far as the Mental Health Officer considers relevant for the purposes of the review, details of the personal circumstances of the patient.

Patient has a history of mental illness dating to 1999 where he was diagnosed with schizophrenia. Patient had hospital-based treatment in B. Unit twice and also supported accommodation in D, from [date] This placement broke down in [date] due to a deterioration in patient's mental health. He was admitted to a psychiatric ward in E hospital and then transferred to a long-term psychiatric ward in F. Hospital on [date].

Patient was re-admitted to C. Unit on [date]. The reviews indicate steady progress. This is mainly due to symptom control with his medication (Clozapine) and also patient's motivation to progress his life. Dr. G. and her staff predict this process will take a long time due to patient's immaturity to manage a more independent live-style.

d) if known to the Mental Health Officer, details of any advance statement that the patient has made (and not withdrawn).

Patient has /has not made an advance statement. I understand patient is satisfied with the care and treatment he gets from the staff in B. Unit. Attached is patient's advance statement dated .... [delete]

e) any other information which the Mental Health Officer considers may assist the Tribunal in considering the determination.

Patient intends to appeal this CTO. I am not sure when this will be given the proximity of the current order. Patient has seen H, solicitor, along with I., Advocacy Worker on .... [date].

f) the social circumstances report, if available.

Social circumstances report dated [date] by J, student Mental Health Officer in medical files.

I understand under the same regulations cited above you are obliged to send a copy of the care plan and this report to the following people –

i) Patient – subject to section 87(3) – , that is, if you thought there would be significant harm to the patient or to others.
ii) Patient's named person – in patient's case not applicable.
iii) Designated Mental Health Officer.

Yours sincerely

....
MHO/Designated MHO

Ⓒ Letter 3: MHO to Independent Advocacy Service reference CTO review

Independent Advocacy Worker
Office address: ....

Date: ....

Dear ....

Re: Notification under section 85(2)(c)[7]/section 89(2)(d)[8] [delete where not applicable] of the Mental Health (Care and Treatment)(Scotland) Act 2003 ["2003 Act"]

Application: section 86 (1) [extend]/section 90(2) [extend and vary]/section 95 [vary] of the 2003 Act. [delete where not applicable]

Subject of application/Community Index Number (where known):

. . . .

. . . .

Subject's current address:

. . . .

Current statute/expiry (where applicable) . . . .

Details of application to extend/vary/extend and vary the compulsory treatment order [delete where not applicable]

. . . .

I am obliged under section 85(2)(c)/section 89(2)(d) to take appropriate steps to ensure that the patient has the opportunity of making use of your services [delete where not applicable]. I have informed the above subject that your service is available for use under section 259 of the 2003 Act.

The following is my understanding of subject's wishes:

[freetext] . . . .

Yours faithfully

....
MHO/Designated MHO

4) Chapter 5: MHO legal duties for review of compulsion order

Summary of letters:

Ⓐ Letter 1 MHO to patient reference compulsion order review

Ⓑ Letter 2 MHO to RMO. Views on review and MHO report for Tribunal (sample)

Ⓒ Letter 3 MHO to Independent Advocacy Services reference compulsion order review

Ⓐ Letter 1: MHO to patient reference compulsion order review

To: ....

Date: ....

Dear Mr/Mrs/Ms ....

Subject: Compulsion order – first/further review to extend and/or vary the powers in the order.

Date of compulsion order (where relevant) ....

Further to your detention I am legally obliged under section 147(2)(b)/151(2)(b)/155(2)(b)/159(4C)(c) [delete where not relevant][9] of the Mental Health (Care and Treatment) (Scotland) Act 2003 (the "2003 Act") to inform you of the following:

You were placed on a compulsion order at .... sheriff court on.. This has to be reviewed before it expires on ....

Dr. ...., your Psychiatrist wishes to review this order to include the following [delete where not applicable]

i) Extend the order by another 6 or 12 months. [delete where not applicable]
ii) Vary the order to include the following measures. [delete where not applicable]
iii) Extend and vary the order

Dr. .... wishes to vary your compulsion order by including the following measures. [delete where not applicable]

1. section 66(1)(a) – detention in a specified hospital - ....
2. section 66(1)(b) – giving of medical treatment under Part 16 of the 2003 Act.
3. section 66(1)(c) – attendance for medical treatment.
4. section 66(1)(d) – attendance to receive community care services.
4. section 66(1)(e) – reside at a specified place – ....
5. section 66(1)(f) – access requirement .
6. section 66(1)(g) – approval of MHO to any proposed change of address.
7. section 66(1)(h) – patient to inform MHO of any change of address.

Dr. .... has to apply/notify[10] to the Mental Health Tribunal for Scotland based in Hamilton, South Lanarkshire to have the measures changed/extended [delete where not relevant]. Both you and ...., your named person have a legal right a) to be heard[11] OR b) apply to revoke the order[12] [delete where not relevant] at a tribunal hearing under section 167/163 [delete where not relevant] of the 2003 Act. You and your named person will be entitled to Legal Aid.

You have the right of an Independent Advocacy Services under Section 259 of the 2003 Act. I have written to this service based in ...., about the application. They will be in contact with you at some point/it is my understanding you do not wish contact. [delete where not applicable]

The following is my understanding of your wishes so far.

[freetext] . . . .

Yours sincerely

....
MHO

cc named person/address (where relevant)

Ⓑ Letter 2: MHO to RMO. Views on CO review and MHO report for Tribunal (sample)

To: Dr X, responsible medical officer

Address: X Hospital

Date: ....

Dear Dr. X

Patient: X.

Current address: . . . .

CHI Number: 12345678910

Social Work computer number: 12345

Review of compulsion order/date (where relevant): X month/year.

1) section 148(2)(a) MHO consultation – first review of a compulsion order.
2) section 152(2)(b) MHO consultation – further mandatory reviews of a compulsion order.
3) section 159(4)(c) MHO consultation – from time to time review to vary a compulsion order.
4) section 182(3)(c) MHO consultation – annual review of a compulsion order with a restriction order.

This is to inform I am discharging my duties under number ( ) above in the Mental Health (Care and Treatment) (Scotland) Act 2003 (the Act), to provide a report in response to your mandatory review consultation.

MHO Duties as follows: [relevant duty in bold]

1. Section 147(2)(d)(i) – MHO's duty to inform RMO whether they agree/disagree with extending client's CTO.
2. Section 151(2)(d) – MHO's duty to inform RMO whether they agree/disagree to extending the CO by 12 months
3. Section 155(2)(e) – MHO's duty to inform the RMO whether they agree or disagree with extending and varying the CO
4. Section 159(4C)(e) – RMO to consult the MHO to vary the CO.

MHO report using headings in the Scottish Statutory Instrument. The Mental Health (compulsion orders – documents and reports to be submitted to the Tribunal) (Scotland) Regulations 2005 No.365. (case example supplied)

(i) on the steps that the Mental Health Officer has taken to comply with the requirements imposed by MHO duty ( ) above;

Joint interview with Dr. X, patient's RMO on [date]
Letter to patient dated [X] informing him of his legal rights to have representation to the tribunal hearing under section 167(6)[13]
Letter to Independent Advocacy Services, dated [X] advising them of this application.

(ii) giving the views of the Mental Health Officer on the application and the reasons for those views;

In agreement with this application/determination[14] [delete]

Reasons:
I would agree the legal criteria under section 139(4)(a) to (c) to extend the order still exist, i.e.

(a) mental disorder – bi-polar disorder;
(b) treatment available – medication, monitoring by community psychiatric nurse [Forensic Unit];
(c) significant risk to health, safety or welfare of patient.

The third criterion is probably the most significant reason to continue with this order. Patient has a chaotic life-style that slips into self-neglect and petty crime to feed his drug misuse. The compulsion order itself is at least a legal attempt to monitor his treatment. I am in agreement however that any future police charges should be dealt with through the normal penal procedures than through this order.

(iii) giving, if known to the Mental Health Officer, the views of the patient and the patient's named person on the application and the reasons for those views;

Patient is aware of this application to extend his compulsion order. I gained the impression that the patient was indifferent as to whether or not the order is extended.

Patient has no nominated or default named person under section 250 or section 251 of the 2003 Act. Patient has three siblings; parents are now deceased; married and divorced with three children, two who are under 18 years. Patient has no contact with any of his immediate or extended family. Patient has no other primary carer.

(iv) giving, in so far as the Mental Health Officer considers relevant for the purposes of the review, details of the personal circumstances of the patient;

Patient was admitted to X. hospital through the court system on [date]. Self involved in supporting this decision and also preparation of a social circumstances report (dated X). Patient had originally been admitted to this ward on [date]. The psychiatric report by you dated X. diagnosed patient as having a bi-polar mental disorder. Patient's psychiatric history dates from [year]. Patient has had fifteen contacts with psychiatrists since [year] to date.

Patient has had a marked forensic history coupled with drug and alcohol misuse. Patient's forensic history has 40 listed charges around some form of aggression to members of the public, including assault, breach of the peace, road traffic act and theft. These are well detailed in your court psychiatric report dated X.

(v) giving, if known to the Mental Health Officer, details of any advance statement the patient has made (and not withdrawn);

Patient has made no advance statement or withdrawn an advance statement. Patient is however satisfied with the treatment he receives. He has a good rapport with his community psychiatric nurse based in the Forensic Unit whom he has known periodically for many years.

(vi) giving any other information which the Mental Health Officer considers may assist the Tribunal in considering the application.

On his recent admission, patient responded well to treatment for his bi-polar illness. You decided to suspend patient's compulsion order from January to April; April to 29 May. These suspensions under section 179[15] of the 2003 Act can continue cumulatively for a period of 9 months, that is, up to September.

Patient has a long history of poor compliance and disinterest in working with professionals. A variation to a community-based compulsion order would not change this. This suspension certificate is probably the least restrictive option available in the 2003 Act.

I would therefore not recommend an interim compulsion order be considered under section 168(2) to seek further evidence to extend and vary the measures.

I understand the Tribunal are legally obliged to hold a hearing under section 167 to consider this review. The tribunal hearing can confirm your recommendation to extend the compulsion order using section 167(1)(a).

Yours sincerely.

....
MHO

Ⓒ Letter 3: MHO to Independent Advocacy Services reference compulsion order review

Independent Advocacy Services
Address

Date: ....

Dear ....

Re: Notification under section 147(2)(c)[16]/section 151(2)(c)[17]/section 155(2)(d)[18] [delete where not applicable] of the Mental Health (Care and Treatment)(Scotland) Act 2003. ["the 2003Act"]

RMO's application: section 149[19]/section 158[20]/section 161[21] of the 2003 Act. [delete where not applicable]; OR RMO's determination under section 150[22] of the 2003 Act – mandatory further reviews.

Subject of application/Community Index Number (where known): ....

Subject's current address: . . . .

Current statute (where applicable) . . . .

Details of application to extend/ vary/extend and vary the compulsion order [delete where not applicable] . . . .

I am obliged under section 147(2)(c)/section 151(2)(c)/section 155(2)(d) to take appropriate steps to ensure that the patient has the opportunity of making use of your services [delete where not applicable]. I have informed the above subject that your service is available for use under section 259 of the 2003 Act.

The following is my understanding of subject's wishes:

[freetext] . . . .

Yours faithfully

....

MHO

5) Chapter 7: Named person

Summary of letters:

Ⓐ **Letter 1** MHO to named person confirming their nomination and appeal rights.

Ⓑ **Letter 2** Named person to MHO declining the nomination.[23]

Ⓒ **Letter 3** MHO to patient's responsible medical officer confirming the patient's named person.[24]

Ⓓ **Letter 4** MHO to Tribunal/Commission reference steps taken to establish a named person, also where the MHO does/does not nominate an alternative named person under section 255(4).

Ⓔ **Letter 5** MHO to Tribunal reference inappropriateness of an apparent named person under section 255(6).

Ⓕ **Letter 6** Named person [nominated or default] writes to the Tribunal requesting no notification and/or to waive their consultation rights for changes in the proposed measures or granting an interim compulsory treatment order.[25]

Ⓐ Letter 1: MHO to named person confirming their nomination and appeal rights

To: .... named person

From: .... Mental Health Officer

Named person's address: ....

Date: ....

Dear Mr/Mrs/Ms ....

Re. Detention of .... under Section .... of the Mental Health (Care and Treatment) (Scotland) Act 2003 (the "2003 Act")

Date /expiry of certificate order (where relevant): ....

Hospital: ....

Psychiatrist/responsible medical officer: ....

I understand the above patient has nominated you as their named person under section 250 **or** you automatically became the named person by default as the primary carer or nearest relative under Section 251 of the above 2003 Act (delete which does not apply).

As named person you have the following rights in relation to the above patient:

1. You will receive written information by the hospital managers about the detention certificate and in more detail about your responsibilities as a named person.
2. You will have an independent right of appeal against the detention order to the Mental Health Tribunal for Scotland, based in Hamilton. You will be entitled to free Legal Aid.
3. The Psychiatrist will consult you if there are any proposed changes to the care plan.

Should you **not** wish to formally act as a named person please sign and return the attached form, addressed to myself.

The following is my understanding of your wishes so far (where relevant)

Freetext: ....

Yours sincerely

....

MHO/Designated MHO

cc RMO; Patient; Health Records, RSNH, Larbert and others (where appropriate)

Ⓑ Letter 2: Named person to MHO declining the nomination

To:

(1) X Council Social Services

Name: . . . .

Mental Health Officer

Address/telephone: . . . .

Subject of civil compulsory powers: [if relevant]

Name: . . . .

Current address: . . . .

Reason for admission/date: [where relevant] . . . .

Home address: . . . .

This is to notify you I **decline** to be nominated as the named person/or default named person [delete which is relevant] for the above person.

I understand I am exercising this right in the Mental Health (Care and Treatment) (Scotland) Act 2003 under one of the following sections.

(1) Section 250(6) where I have been formally nominated by the nominator cited above.
(2) Section 251(6) where I am the default named person as a result of being the primary carer of the person cited above.
(3) Section 254(5) where I am the default named person as a result of being the nearest relative of the person cited above under section 254 of the 2003 Act. [delete which is not relevant]
(4) Section 257(2) – appointment as named person by the Tribunal.

Yours sincerely

Print full name/address: . . . .

Date: ....

Copy to: . . . .

Person subject to civil compulsory powers. [where relevant]

Letter 3: MHO to patient's responsible medical officer confirming the patient's named person

To: .... responsible medical officer

Address: ....

Date: ....

Dear Dr. ....

Subject: .... d.o.b. ....

Address: ....

Certificate/date (where relevant) ....

This is to inform you I am discharging my duties under Section 45(3)(b)/section 59/section 255 [delete where not relevant] of the Mental Health (Care and Treatment) (Scotland) Act 2003 (the 2003 Act), to identify the following person as the above patient's named person.

Name: ....

Address: ....

Telephone: ....

The named person was nominated by the patient under Section 250 of the 2003 Act/or acting as the default named person under Section 251 of the 2003 Act, that is, primary carer/nearest relative; / decision of tribunal hearing under section 257(2). (delete where not appropriate)

OR:

I was unable to establish the patient's named person for the following reasons –

1. Nominated/default named person has declined the nomination under section 251(6) [primary carer declines]/section 254(5) [nearest relative declines] or: Attached is a copy of this notification declining their nomination. [delete where not relevant]
2. Named person refused to decline in writing. Self declaring them inappropriate under section 255(6) as a result of their refusal/other reasons [delete where not relevant]
3. Patient has made a declaration stating they do not want their primary carer/nearest relative to be the named person. Attached is copy of patient's declaration.

4. Self unable to identify any named person for the following reasons –

   Freetext: ....

In accordance with the Code of Practice on the 2003 Act [ref: volume 1; chapter six, paragraph 34; page 91] I will send a copy of this letter to the following agencies/people

1. Health Records Department, X Hospital
2. Charge Nurse – ward X
3. Patient
4. Independent Advocacy Service [supply office address]
5. Named person X
6. ....
7. ....

Yours sincerely

....
Designated MHO

Ⓓ Letter 4: MHO to Tribunal/Commission reference steps taken to establish a named person, also where the MHO does/does not nominate an alternative named person under section 255(4)

Duty Convener
First Floor
Bothwell House
Hamilton Business Park
Caird Park
Hamilton
ML3 0QA

Date:

Dear Sir/Madam,

Subject of application: ....

Tribunal reference/CHI number (if known): ....

Current address: [insert ward + full postal address] ....

Compulsory treatment order date of application ....

I am obliged under section 255(4) of the Mental Health (Care and Treatment) (Scotland) Act 2003 to inform the Tribunal/Mental Welfare Commission of the steps I took to establish whether the patient has a named person. I am expected to do this as soon as practicable.

Steps taken to establish a named person.

1. Established patient had not nominated a named person under section 250.
2. Established the default named person would be patient's mother [example].
3. Inspected medical case notes – which showed long-standing conflict between patient/mother [example].

   ....

   Spoke to patient twice who confirmed she did not want her mother nominated as named person. [example]

Additional information: section 255(4) – substitute nomination

I understand I have discretion under section 255(4)(b) to make an application for an alternative named person. I recommend the person below to be made the named person for the following reason. [example]

Proposed named person: Ms. X, friend.

1) Ms. X. has known patient for many years and has offered friendship and support throughout patient's illnesses.
2) Ms. X. impresses as a caring person. Ms. X. visits patient regularly in the ward. The nursing staff note that patient seems to benefit from these visits.
3) I have discussed the role of named person with Ms. X. and also given published information. Ms. X. is willing to take on the named person role.
4) Ms. X. will be present at patient's tribunal hearing to answer questions.

OR:

I understand I have discretion under section 255(4)(b) to make an application for an alternative named person. I chose **not** to do so for the following reason. [example]

1) I understand patient has little contact with her two siblings in Scotland. They have not visited patient since her admission. The nursing staff have tried to contact one of the sisters but without success.
2) I would prefer to leave the nomination of a named person (if any) to the patient once she has recovered capacity. This would be in harmony with the section 1 principle of patient's past and present wishes.
3) The other pragmatic reason is patient is too unwell for me to consult her about alternative nominations.

Yours sincerely

....

Designated Mental Health Officer

cc Mental Welfare Commission for Scotland
Dr X, responsible medical officer

Ⓔ Letter 5: MHO to Tribunal reference inappropriateness of an apparent named person under section 255(6)

Duty Convener
First Floor, Bothwell House
Hamilton Business Park
Caird Park
Hamilton ML3 0QA

Date: ....

Dear Sir/Madam,

Subject of application: . . . .

Tribunal reference/Community Health Index number (if known): . . . .

Address: [insert full postal address] c/o: Ward X.

Compulsory treatment order date of application: . . . .

I am obliged to inform the Tribunal/Mental Welfare Commission under section 255(6) & (7) of the Mental Health (Care and Treatment) (Scotland) Act 2003 to apply to a Tribunal for an order under section 257(2) where an apparent named person is declared not to be the named person on the grounds of being inappropriate.

Reasons for this application: (example)

1) I understand patient has little contact with her apparent named person. She has not visited patient since her admission. The nursing staff have tried to contact the apparent named person on several occasions and have been met with a hostile response, suggesting lack of interest.
2) I have also contacted the apparent named person and been met with a similar response. The apparent named person refuses to sign a prepared letter to the local authority declining her role as default named person.
3) I would prefer to leave the nomination of a named person (if any) to the patient once she has recovered capacity. This would be in harmony with the section 1 principle of patient's past and present wishes. The other pragmatic reason is patient is too unwell for me to consult her about alternative nominations.

Yours sincerely

....
Designated Mental Health Officer

cc Mental Welfare Commission for Scotland
Dr. X, RMO

F Letter 6: Named person [nominated or default] writes to the Tribunal requesting no notification and/or to waive their consultation rights for changes in the proposed measures or granting an interim compulsory treatment order.

Duty Convener
First Floor, Bothwell House
Hamilton Business Park
Caird Park
Hamilton ML3 0QA

Date: ....

Dear Sir/Madam,

Subject of application: ....

My relation to subject: ....

Tribunal reference/CHI number (if known): ....

Current address: c/o: Ward ....., Hospital address ....

Compulsory treatment order date of application (if known) ....

Mental Health Officer/address: ....

I am obliged to put in writing the following requests for the Tribunal on any future hearings about the above subject. [tick options]

1. I accept the nomination of named person under section 251(5) of the Mental Health (Care and Treatment)(Scotland) Act 2003, that is, nomination by patient under section 250 Or default nomination as primary care/nearest relative under section 251. [delete where appropriate]
2. I do **not** wish to be present at the review or receive any notification of any hearings.[26]
3. I do **not** wish to appeal the result of any hearings.
4. I wish to **waive my right of appeal** should the Tribunal decide to change the measures in the proposed care plan in the compulsory treatment order application as stated in section 64(7) – change of measures; section 65(4) – making of an interim compulsory treatment order.

Yours sincerely

....
Print full name/address

Footnotes:

1 The MHO need only write Letter 1 after giving/not giving consent. CoP, vol 2, chapter 7, para 45, p. 195.
2 This is a simple template deliberately to allow for elaboration.
3 In writing to the independent advocacy services, the MHO is proving they are taking appropriate steps to ensure that the patient has the opportunity of making use of those services [section 61(2)(d)].
4 Oddly the MHO has no legal duty to inform the named person of reviews although it would be good practice to do so.
5 Tribunal powers on an RMO's application to extend and/or vary a CTO [s.92/95]; or a patient/named person to have a CTO revoked or varied [s. 99/100] In any kind of application, a patient/named person has a right to be given the opportunity to have legal representation or leading or producing evidence.
6 The RMO has to consult the MHO and also seek their views about agreement or disagreement. This was amended by the Scottish Statutory Instrument 2004 No. 533 with sections 4(A) to 4(E) being inserted after section 93(4).
7 Extension of a CTO.
8 Extending and varying a CTO.
9 The MHO may wish to give a brief explanation at this stage what the section means , that is, s. 147 – extend for 6 months; s. 151 – extend for 12 months; s. 155 – extend and vary for either 6 or 12 months; s. 159 – to vary the order.
10 Applications refer to the first review and any review that extends and/or varies the compulsion order. Notifications, or more accurately "determinations", refer only to further mandatory reviews to extend the compulsion order by 12 months. The latter does not require a tribunal hearing.
11 A patient/named person's right to be heard occurs when a tribunal hearing is held.
12 Patient/named person can apply to the Tribunal to have an extended compulsion order revoked or the measures varied under section 164. In other words, the compulsion order has firstly to be extended before an application can be made. This can be done by either a tribunal hearing or an RMO's determination.
13 section 167 lists the types of reviews a Tribunal has to consider on application by either an RMO [s. 149/158/161 or a patient/named person [s. 163/164].
14 Determination only applies in the further mandatory reviews for 12-month periods. The Tribunal through administration usually ratifies them. Applications are always decided by a tribunal hearing.
15 section 179 are suspensions for criminal proceedings orders. This section is x-referenced with sections 127/128/129 [suspension of civil orders] where the same conditions apply.
16 First review extension by six months. This is decided by a tribunal hearing.
17 Further mandatory review by RMO – 12 month periods.
18 Extension and variation for either six months or 12 months. Decided by Tribunal.
19 Application is first review to extend the compulsion order by 6 months.
20 Application in any review – extension and variation of compulsion order.
21 Application to vary the compulsion order – "time to time" reviews.
22 Determination – RMO's paperwork to the Tribunal to extend the CO to 12 months.
23 Named person can decline [s. 250(6); primary carer [s. 251(6); nearest relative [s. 254(5)].
24 MHO duties) short-term certificate [s. 45(1)(b)]; CTO application [s. 59]; after a compulsion order has been made [s. 138]; after a compulsion order and a restriction order is made [s. 181]; after a hospital direction or a transfer for

treatment direction has been made [s. 205].

25 Tribunal Rule No 56(2) requesting no notifications from the Tribunal about a hearing. Section 65(4) – waive rights of consultation before the Tribunal make an interim CTO.

26 Tribunal Rule 56(2). The Rules are in the Scottish Statutory Instrument 2005 No.519.

Appendix 1

Glossary of terms and abbreviations

Note: All legal references are to sections in the Mental Health (Care and Treatment) (Scotland) Act 2003 [abbreviated to 'the Act' below] with page numbers in brackets, unless otherwise stated.

Advance statement

[section 275, page 199]

This is a written statement from any person, including children, in advance about their medical treatment should they be detained under the Act. The statement has to be countersigned by a prescribed witness to confirm capacity at the time of writing the statement.

Any medical practitioner and the Tribunal have to try to follow the advance statement. If there is conflict in the statement with treatment, this must be recorded and sent to relevant parties, including the Mental Welfare Commission.

Approved medical practitioner [AMP]

[section 22, page 13]

This is a medical practitioner with specialist training in psychiatry. They are accredited by their Health Trusts before being authorised to apply the Act. They can detain a person on a short-term detention certificate [28 days] and also write a Mental Health Report for a compulsory treatment order (CTO) and criminal proceedings orders.

Assessment order

[section 130; subsection 52D, page 80]

A pre-disposal order made by the court under section 52D of the Criminal Procedure (Scotland) Act 1995 authorising hospital detention for up to 28 days so the patient's mental condition may be assessed. This section is inserted into the Act under section 130.

Authorised person's warrant

[section 292, page 213]

This allows an authorised person, for example, a nurse or an MHO, to enter a patient's home and return them to hospital. This could apply to a patient who has absconded from hospital and is refusing entry. The person must already be detained under an order in the Act. A police constable would be authorised to force entry where necessary.

Care plan

[section 76, page 48]

This is a record prepared by the patient's RMO after the Tribunal has granted a compulsory treatment order. It describes the medical and/or community care services the patient will receive whilst under this order. A care plan differs from a *"proposed care plan"* which is written by a Mental Health Officer as part of an application for a compulsory treatment order [see below].

Community mental health team [CMHT]

A multi-disciplinary team providing care, treatment and community-based services to a patient. They are normally made up of medical practitioners; community psychiatric nurses; social workers and occupational therapists.

Community psychiatric nurse [CPN]

A qualified nurse who delivers the majority of their care to a patient within a community setting.

Compulsion order [CO]

[section 133, subsection 57A, page 100]

A mental health disposal made by the court authorising compulsory measures (either hospital or community-based) initially for a period of six months. A Tribunal can only renew it.

Compulsory treatment order [CTO]

[section 64(4), page 42] – see Chapter 3

An order granted by the Tribunal. It authorises any of the compulsory measures listed at section 66(1) in the Act. It initially lasts for six months, and can be renewed for another six months and then annually. It can also be stopped by a patient's RMO at any time.

Designated medical practitioner [DMP]

[section 233, page 165]

A specialist in psychiatry who is appointed by the Mental Welfare Commission to provide a second medical opinion with respect to certain treatments given in Part 16 of the Act.

Emergency detention certificate [EDC]

[section 36, page 22] – see Chapter 2

A certificate completed by any medical practitioner that can detain either an informal patient or a community-based patient in any hospital for up to 72 hours. The five legal criteria are based on a *"likelihood"* test. It is not appealable. If the person is in the community, the certificate authorises that person to be removed to hospital within 72 hours of the certificate being completed. An MHO is usually involved in giving consent although this can be waived if it is impracticable to do so [section 36(6)].

Extension certificate

[section 47(1), page 30]

A certificate issued by an approved medical practitioner that extends a period of short-term detention – in itself 28 days – by a further 3 working days to allow for the preparation of an application for a CTO. This is only done if there has been deterioration in a patient's mental health towards the end of the short-term detention.

General Practitioner [GP]

A fully registered medical practitioner providing primary care services within a community based practice. They can complete 3-day emergency certificates only.

Hospital direction

section 59A of the Criminal Procedure (Scotland) Act 1995

A mental health court disposal made in addition to a sentence of imprisonment. It allows the convicted person to be detained in hospital for treatment of their mental disorder and then transferred to prison to complete their sentence once detention in hospital is no longer required.

Independent advocate

[section 259, page 181]

A paid person who enables a patient to express their views about their care and treatment. They can also be a voice for the patient if the patient is unable to speak for him or herself. All people with mental disorders have a right to independent advocacy, not only those subject to compulsory measures.

Interim compulsion order

[section 131, subsection 53, page 95] (inserted as section 53 of the Criminal Procedure (Scotland) Act 1995)

A pre-disposal court order authorising a mentally disordered offender to be detained in hospital initially for 12 weeks. This can be continued at 12-weekly intervals for up to one year. It usually applies to serious offences with a view to imposing a restriction order. The Scottish Executive monitors it.

Interim compulsory treatment order

[section 65(2), page 44]

A care and treatment order granted by a Tribunal. It authorises compulsory measures for a period of up to 28 days at a time but no more than a total of 56 days. It can be either hospital or community based. It can be suspended for hospital treatment only.

Medical treatment

[section 329, page 242]

Treatment for a mental disorder. This includes nursing, care, psychological intervention, habilitation (including education, and training in work, social and independent living skills) and rehabilitation –

skills already acquired but lost or impaired due to the effect of the mental disorder.

The term *"medical treatment"* includes giving medication as well as other physical interventions, such as electro-convulsive therapy (ECT), in addition to psychological and social interventions made with respect to mental disorder.

Mental Health Officer [MHO]

[section 32, page 18]

Officers of the local authority (social workers) who meet certain requirements on qualifications, training, experience and competence with people who have a mental disorder. They are the only professionals who can give consent to detentions and also apply for a CTO.

Mental Welfare Commission for Scotland

[section 4, page 4]

An independent organisation set up by Parliament responsible for protecting the welfare of people with mental disorder including learning disability in Scotland. They inquire into cases of ill-treatment or deficiency of care and treatment, and visit patients in hospital and in the community. These duties apply regardless of where the individual lives. They are currently based in Edinburgh.

Contact details: Tel: 0131 222 6111, Website: www.mwcscot.org.uk

Named person

[section 250, page 174] – see Chapter 7

This is anyone over the age of 16 nominated by another person to protect their interests should they ever be detained. This could be, for example, a close friend, a partner or a relative. If no nomination has been made at the point of detention, there is a default position, firstly the person's primary carer, then nearest relative. The named person is entitled to receive medical information about the detained patient. The named person has a right to be consulted by the medical practitioner and can also act independently to appeal certain detentions.

Nearest relative

[section 254(2)(a) to (j), page 177]

This is a detained person's legal family aged over 16 years of age, listed in nine categories, that is, from spouse to niece, with full-blood relatives being a priority. The elder or eldest of any group, for example, siblings, is usually the nearest relative if there is a disagreement about nomination. Where the detained person has no relatives but has lived with another person for more than five years, that person would be termed the nearest relative. The nearest relative has to be ordinarily resident in the United Kingdom, the Channel Islands or the Isle of Man. The nearest relative, if living with the detained person, has to be notified when that person is admitted to hospital under an EDC. They and any relative of the patient have a right to object to a named person's nomination. Their rights are curtailed in favour of a named person.

Nurse's holding power

[section 299, page 219]

This is a power open to all registered mental or learning disability nurses to hold/detain a person already in a psychiatric hospital for up to two hours. This applies to a voluntary patient, or a person receiving in-patient or outpatient psychiatric treatment while under a probation order. The nurse has to consider whether it is likely that the held patient meets the five legal tests needed to apply either an emergency or a short-term detention certificate. The *"holding period"* is used to access a medical practitioner and MHO where they are not immediately available. There is a further hour allowed for the examination to take place.

Place of safety

[section 300, page 220]

This is where a person can be taken by the police from their home or in the community for periods from 24 hours, 72 hours or 7 days, depending on the type of warrant or order. The Act defines a place of safety as a hospital, a care home service or any other suitable place, other than a police station, where the occupier is willing to temporarily receive a person with a mental disorder. A police station would only be used as a place of safety if no other place were available. The purpose of holding a person is usually for a medical examination, so the duration would be as short as possible.

Proposed care plan

[section 62, page 39]

This is a document prepared by an MHO as part of a CTO application to a Tribunal. It contains details of the recommended medical treatment for mental disorder; the community care services; and any other forms of care and treatment. The Tribunal can change this proposed care plan according to the evidence heard.

Recorded matters

[section 64(4)(ii), page 43]

These are particular types of medical treatment, community care services, relevant services or any other form of treatment, care or service, which the Tribunal wishes to mark out as being essential to a care package. The legal test for imposing recorded matters is *"reasonableness"*. The patient's RMO and the Mental Welfare Commission can make a reference to the Tribunal if these recorded matters are not being met. The Tribunal then have powers to modify the recorded matters and/or modifying or revoking the CTO [section 96, section 98 & section 104].

Registered mental nurse [RMN]

A qualified nurse under Part 3 of the register held by the Nursing and Midwifery Council who specialises in the provision and care of people with mental health problems.

Removal order

[section 293(1), page 214] – see Chapter 6

An order granted by a sheriff or a justice of the peace [*"justice"*] to an MHO on application. It authorises an MHO along with a police constable and any other specified person, say, a medical practitioner, to enter the home of a person over the age of 16, who has already been diagnosed as having a mental disorder and who is deemed to be at risk.

The warrant is valid for 72 hours and can be used to take this person to a place of safety for up to 7 days. The warrant allows any police constable to forcibly open the premises if access is denied.

The risk applies to self-neglect, ill-treatment; living alone or without care; unable to look after himself or his property or financial affairs; risk to their property. The medical practitioner may be present to examine and complete a civil compulsory order. This is usually the case, as the removal order does not allow medical treatment.

Responsible medical officer [RMO]

[section 230, page 163]

A fully registered medical practitioner who must be an AMP appointed to assess and supervise a detained patient's medical care and treatment. They have to be appointed by the hospital managers after an *"appropriate act"*/detention occurs. This includes *"a relevant event"*. There are nine such events listed in section 232, including civil and criminal powers. The most common application is after a short-term detention certificate [see 'Social circumstances report' below for list of relevant events].

Restricted patient

[section 133 subsection 57A (7), page 102]

A patient who has been made subject to a compulsion order and a restriction order by the court. They have usually committed a serious offence. They can remain in hospital for an indefinite period of time (see below).

Restriction order

[section 133 subsection 57A (7), page 102]

An order made by the court under section 59 of the Criminal Procedure (Scotland) Act 1995 at the time of disposal and is added to a compulsion order. It means that the measures specified in the compulsion order will be without limit of time. Some of these patients are detained in the State Hospital. They are however still subject to reviews by a shrieval panel, consisting of a sheriff, sheriff principal or a part-time sheriff.

Senior House Officer [SHO] – Speciality Training grades 1, 2 or 3

A fully registered medical practitioner working within a medical speciality as part of their training. They can complete an EDC regardless of their speciality, for example, Accident & Emergency or in any hospital wards.

Short-term detention certificate

[section 44(1), page 27]

This is a certificate that authorises the detention of a person in hospital for up to 28 days for care and treatment. An approved medical practitioner can grant this but only with consent from an MHO. The patient and named person can appeal this certificate together or separately [section 50].

Social circumstances report

[section 231, page 164]

A report completed by the MHO. It must be done within 21 days of a *"relevant event"*, that is, an order imposed by a doctor/Tribunal or the courts. These relevant events are as follows:

- Short-term detention certificate [s. 44, p. 27]
- Interim compulsory treatment order [s. 65, p. 44]
- Compulsory treatment order [s. 64(4), p. 42]
- Assessment order [s. 130 ss.52D, p. 80]
- Treatment order [s. 130 ss.52M; p. 88]
- Interim compulsion order [s. 131 ss.53 (8), p. 96]
- Compulsion order [s. 133 ss 57A(2) p. 101]
- Hospital direction [s. 59A of the 1995 Act]
- Transfer for treatment direction [s. 136, p. 136]

Social Worker [SW]

An officer of the local authority who has achieved appropriate qualifications and experience in the assessment and delivery of social care needs.

Specialist Registrar [SpR] – Speciality Training grades 4, 5 or 6

A fully registered medical practitioner who has achieved further qualifications within their chosen field of medical practice.

Transfer for treatment direction

[section 136, page 108]

An order that is made by the Scottish Ministers, which allows the transfer of a sentenced prisoner for care and treatment to a psychiatric hospital The transfer can also be to the State Hospital.

Treatment order

[section 130, subsection 52 M, page 88]

A pre-disposal order made by the court authorising hospital detention for treatment of a person's mental disorder. The order ceases at the end of the period for which the person is on remand or is committed.

Tribunal

[section 21, page 13]

This is called The Mental Health Tribunal for Scotland, based in Hamilton, Scotland. They have replaced the sheriff court system to consider applications for CTOs, appeals and reviews of various orders. The Tribunal has a 3-panel membership made up of legal/medical/general members. The legal member is called the Convener who chairs the Tribunal.

Contact details: Mental Health Tribunal for Scotland
First Floor, Bothwell House,
Hamilton Business Park, Caird Park,
Hamilton Ml3 0QA
Tel: 01698 390000
Website: www.mhtscot.gov.uk

Warrants

[section 35, page 20]

Section 35 warrants: these are warrants issued by a sheriff or a justice of the peace on an application from an MHO. There are three kinds:

(1) to enter premises;

(2) to detain a person for a medical examination for up to 3 hours; and

(3) to allow a medical practitioner access to a person's medical records where consent cannot be given. There is no right of appeal against a warrant being granted or not granted.

Appendix 2

What happens after the MHO has given consent

1) Subsequent events after an emergency certificate is granted

1. Medical Practitioner completes Part 1 of Form DET 1

- The medical practitioner has to complete Part 1 of Form DET 1. The hospital managers or a ward-based representative has to complete Part 2.
- The timescale to complete and sign the certificate depends when the medical examination ends, that is, after the MHO has given consent. The Act restricts the time to fours hours' minimum for the certificate to be signed. The critical clock time is therefore any time from 8pm to 12 midnight whereby the medical practitioner then only has four hours to complete the certificate.
- Effectively the examination itself can take any length of time. The legal timescales only apply when the examination is complete with MHO consent given. The Form DET 1 makes this helpful distinction, that is, when the examination was completed and the form signed.[1]
- The legal reference for completing this form is section 37. This form is a means of the medical practitioner "*giving notice*" [quote] to the hospital managers. The Act suggests that separate notice be given but the Form DET 1 already covers the detention issues listed in section 37. Form DET 1 is effectively the certificate.

2. Patient already in hospital [section 36(11)]

- If the patient is already in hospital the detention period starts as soon as the certificate is given to the hospital managers or a ward-based representative.[2]
- The manager/representative has to record in Part 2 of Form DET 1 the exact time and date the 72-hour detention period began and when it is due to expire.

3. Patient not in hospital – transfer arrangements [section 36 (8)(a)]

- The authority to use the EDC is valid for up to 72 hours after the medical practitioner signs the certificate.
- The Code of Practice states that the medical practitioner, and not the MHO, would be responsible for the organisation of the transfer.[3]

4. Admit patient [section 36(8)(b)(i)]

- The patient cannot be formally detained for up to 72 hours until the hospital manager or the ward-based representative receives the Form DET 1 emergency certificate.
- The hospital managers have to complete the record of admission in Part 2, that is, the name of the hospital, ward/date and time when the detention began and expires.[4]
- The Code of Practice suggests it would be good practice for allocation of a named nurse at the point of admission.[5]

5. Appoint an approved medical practitioner [AMP] [section 38(2)]

- This certificate allows for a safeguard against wrongful detention given there is no right of appeal.
- The hospital managers have to make arrangements for an AMP – usually a Consultant Psychiatrist – to examine the patient. There is no specific timetable but the Act phrases it as follows "as *soon as practicable after the period of detention begins*".
- The timescale for re-examination is short to allow for a more thorough examination by a specialist.
- The patient's detention may have to be reviewed by any psychiatrist, say, out of hours or at weekends, hence the distinction between an AMP and a "*responsible medical officer*" [RMO], who is allocated after the patient is placed on a short-term detention certificate. See 'Subsequent events after a short-term certificate is granted' below.
- The options for the AMP are to revoke the certificate[6]; allow it to run the full 72 hours[7]; suspend it for any period up to 72 hours (unlikely);[8]

complete a short-term detention certificate which would come into effect the same day it was signed.[9]

- The important issue is to have the patient examined and, if necessary, monitored, for a period of up to 72 hours before any of the above options are used. It would still be least restrictive and beneficial if the detained patient were not progressed onto another certificate as a result of a comprehensive assessment by the AMP. This could apply to, say, patients with a drug-induced psychosis or acute confusional state where their symptoms would improve within a 72-hour period. The AMP and MHO should, therefore, not automatically leap to a short-term certificate that restricts the patient's liberty for up to 28 days.

6. Hospital Managers have to inform the patient's nearest relative and/or the named person, if known [section 38(3)(a)]

- The hospital managers must do this within 12 hours of the patient's admission under an EDC. This would usually be by telephone. The full list of those informed is as follows:[10]

  i) Patient's nearest relative as defined in section 254(1) of the Act. This notification only applies if they are actually living with the person who has been detained.
  ii) Any person who resides with the patient if the patient's nearest relative does not reside with the patient.
  iii) The patient's named person, if known, and not one of the above.
  iv) The Mental Welfare Commission by telephone on 0131 222 6111.

The hospital manager or ward-based representative has to record under "*Record of Notice Given*" on Form DET 1, page 6, the names of the people informed.[11]

7. Written notification about the detention [section 38(3)(b)]

- The hospital manager has to notify those listed above, in writing, within 7 days of receiving the certificate of the following details:

  i) the reasons for granting the certificate;
  ii) whether MHO consent was obtained;
  iii) if granted without MHO consent, the reasons why it was impracticable;
  iv) the alternatives to granting the certificate that were considered by the medical practitioner; and
  v) the reason for the medical practitioner determining that any such alternatives were inappropriate.

- A copy of the certificate must be sent to the Mental Welfare Commission.
- If the certificate was granted without MHO consent, the hospital managers have to notify the local authority where the patient lives. If the patient's address is unknown, the local authority where the hospital is situated is notified.[12]
- These notifications must be recorded under "*Record of Notice Given*" in Part 2, Form DET 1.

8. Hospital Managers have to record that they have fulfilled their obligations under section 260 of the 2003 Act – relevant matters

- The Hospital Managers have to send notification in writing to the patient, with a copy to their named person, about the following "*relevant matters*" relating to the detention:

  i) The provision in the Act whereby the patient is detained;
  ii) The consequences of the operation of that provision;
  iii) The powers of the RMO and the Tribunal in relation to revoking the order;
  iv) Any appeal rights, if applicable;
  v) The power of the Tribunal in dealing with these rights;
  vi) How the patient may exercise that right;

vii) The functions of the Mental Welfare Commission in that order;
viii) How the patient may obtain legal assistance to exercise that right.

This is recorded under "*Completion Details*" in Part 2, Form DET 1.

9. AMP revokes the certificate and completes Form REV 1 [section 39(a)] page 25

• If the criteria are not met, the AMP has to complete Form REV 1. This is a general-purpose revocation form covering emergency/ short-term and extension certificates. It is divided into three parts as follows:

Part 1	Revocation of certificate; patient's post-Detention Status.
Part 2	Notification by the Hospital Managers (for emergency certificates only).
Part 3	Termination of detention listing eight ways this can be done, that is, expiry of certificate; revocation by AMP; revocation by Commission; revocation by the Tribunal; transfer out of Scotland; unauthorised absence[13]; death of patient; termination for other reasons.

10. Hospital manager's notification of revocation [section 40(2)]

- After receiving Form REV 1 from the AMP or RMO, the hospital manager has to notify the same people listed in **6.** above and complete Part 3 of the same form.
- The hospital managers must send a copy of Form REV 1 to the Mental Welfare Commission and the Mental Health Tribunal headquarters.

2) Subsequent events after a short-term certificate is granted

1.(a) Patient already in hospital [section 44(5)(b)(ii)]

- If the patient is already in hospital the detention period then starts as soon as the certificate is given to the hospital managers or a ward-based representative.
- If the patient is detained under an EDC this is immediately revoked when the short-term detention certificate is signed. The AMP has to tick the sentence "*the patient was detained in hospital when this, short-term certificate was granted*" in Form DET 2, Part 2.[14]
- The manager/representative has to record on Form DET 2 the date the 28-day detention period began and when it is due to expire. The form states: "*unless revoked or extended, this authorisation will cease at midnight at the end of the 28th day".*[15]

1.(b) Patient not in hospital – transfer arrangements [section 44 (5)(a)]

- The AMP has three days to arrange a hospital admission after the certificate is signed.
- This certificate has to be passed to the hospital managers before a patient is formally admitted and the detention period begins.[16]
- The hospital manager or a ward-based representative has to complete Form DET 2, Part 2, which details the date of admission and the date of expiry.

2. Hospital managers notify parties [section 46(2)]

- The hospital manager has to notify the following parties as soon as practicable when the detention begins and the expected expiry date of the certificate:

  – the patient;
  – the patient's named person
  – any guardian of the patient *
  – any welfare attorney of the patient *

* Guardian and welfare attorney are defined in the Adults with Incapacity (Scotland) Act 2000 – section 64(1)(a) or (b); section 16.

- The Code of Practice suggests that "*best practice*" would be for these parties to have oral notification, for example, by telephone, before letters are sent.[17]
- Section 260(5) obliges the hospital managers to send information to the patient and the named person about "*relevant matters*" as listed below:

    i) the section of the 2003 Act under which the patient is detained.
    ii) the consequences of the order.
    iii) the powers of the RMO and the Tribunal in revoking the order.
    iv) any right to make an application, or appeal, to the Tribunal the patient has.
    v) the powers of the Tribunal if this application/appeal is made.
    vi) how the patient may exercise that right.
    vii) the functions of the Mental Welfare Commission relevant to the order.
    viii) how the patient may obtain legal assistance to appeal the order if appropriate.

These notifications must be recorded under "Record of Notice Given" in Part 2, Form DET 2.

3. Hospital Managers have to copy Form DET 2 to the Mental Welfare Commission and to the Tribunal [section 46(3)(b)]

- A full copy of Form DET 2 has to be sent to the Mental Welfare Commission and the Tribunal headquarters within 7 days of the order being granted. The date this form is sent has to be recorded in Part 2, Form DET 2.[18]

4. Hospital Managers have to appoint a responsible medical officer [RMO] [section 230 (4)(a), x-ref: section 232 (a)]

- The appointed RMO would be a psychiatrist working in the same hospital where the patient is detained. The Act states this appointment has to be made "*as soon as is reasonably practicable.*" The Code of Practice suggests within one working day.[19]
- If a detained patient is in a general hospital receiving, say, surgical treatment, the RMO must be a Psychiatrist. The surgeon cannot discharge the patient without this detention order first being revoked by the RMO.
- Hospital managers need to have interim arrangements in place if the appointed RMO is for any reason unavailable.[20]

5. RMO must examine the patient[21] [section 49(1)]

- There is a duty for the RMO to review the detention *"from time to time"* and assess whether the certificate is still legally valid. The legal test is the RMO's satisfaction as to whether or not the detention criteria under section 44(4) are still met.
- If the RMO thinks it is still necessary for the certificate he has to state this in the Form REV 1 and then go on to complete the options listed in Part 3 (this is the same list as outlined in point 9. on page 231).
- The RMO is not legally obliged to consult an MHO when reviewing a certificate. They only have to inform the MHO in writing of any decisions made.

6(a) RMO decides to revoke the short-term detention certificate [section 49 (2) & (3) & (4)]

- If the criteria for the detention are no longer met, the RMO must revoke the certificate. This involves completing Part 1 of Form REV 1.

6(b) The RMO does not revoke the short-term detention certificate [section 49(1)]

- The RMO has two choices:
  (1) To allow detention to run its full 28 day period and then expire.
  Result: patient can be discharged or remain in the ward voluntarily.
  (2) Proceed to a compulsory treatment order [CTO] application.
  Result: the patient is formally detained for up to 28 days.

- Before the certificate expires, the RMO and the hospital managers must complete Part 3, Form REV 1, ticking off the option "*expiry of authority to detain*".

7. Hospital Managers record when the certificate was terminated [section 46(2) & (3)]

- The hospital managers will already have notified certain parties of the granting of the certificate and also the formal expiry date if the certificate was not revoked or extended.
- Part 3. The hospital managers have to record from a list of possibilities why the certificate was terminated, that is, in this case, " *expiry without authority to detain"* (this is the same list as outlined in point 9. on page 231).
- A copy of Form REV 1 has to be sent to the Mental Welfare Commission and the Tribunal headquarters.

8. Proceed to a CTO Application [section 57(1)]

3) Subsequent events after a CTO is granted

1. Tribunal considers the application/convene tribunal hearing

- When the Tribunal receive the CTO application they have to make one of the following decisions:[22]

– refuse the application;
– grant a CTO; or
– grant an interim CTO

- The Tribunal can compel any person to attend the tribunal hearing and produce evidence. Sanctions can be imposed for non-compliance, without reasonable excuse, with a request to attend or produce evidence for any hearing. Failure to attend a citation would be a criminal offence [2003 Act, Schedule 2(1) p. 254].
- The Tribunal can still proceed in the absence of any individual. It would be for the Tribunal panel to decide whether to proceed with or postpone the hearing in the event of one of more of the attendees not turning up.[23]
- The Tribunal will need 7 days to administer applications to allow them time to send notifications to the parties. The Tribunal HQ's will then decide on the basis of the information whether to hold an oral or a paper hearing. The Tribunal would still have to sit as a formal Tribunal in either case.[24]

2. Application for an Interim CTO [section 65(2)]

- The Act in section 65(2) states that "*on the application of any person having an interest in the proceedings, or ex proprio motu* [at their own discretion], *the Tribunal may make an interim compulsory treatment order"*. The CTO application has to be lodged first by the MHO.[25] This further application can be lodged at the same time as or before the first hearing is arranged.[26]

3. Tribunal considers an application for an Interim CTO [section 65(2)]

- If a patient is already detained under a short-term certificate and the Tribunal have extended this period for up to five working days to allow for a hearing to be arranged using section 68, the first hearing are obliged to consider, before deciding on the CTO application itself, whether an interim CTO should be made.[27]

- The reasons for considering an Interim CTO may be as follows:[28]

  a) Patient already detained under section 68 (see above).
  b) Insufficient information in the application to grant a full 6-month CTO.
  c) The patient's legal representative may require further time to prepare their evidence.
  d) An interested person may have made an application for an Interim CTO.[29]

- The conditions that must be met to grant an Interim CTO are similar to a full CTO. The term "*necessary*" applies in a different context to each order. CTO: "*that the making of the CTO is necessary*", that is, the necessity relates to the interim period and not six months.[30]
- If an Interim CTO is granted, whatever legal preparation is required should only take up to a maximum of 56 days.[31]
- The norm for Interim CTOs are 28 days or less, followed by extensions for specific reasons.[32]
- Before making an Interim CTO, the Tribunal have to allow the following parties the opportunity to make representations (orally or in writing); and lead or produce evidence:
  Patient, named person, guardian of patient, welfare attorney of patient, MHO, AMP/GP, RMO [if different to AMP], patient's primary carer and any *Curator ad litem* appointed by the Tribunal; "*any other person appearing to the Tribunal to have an interest in the application.*"[33]

4. Tribunal grants an Interim CTO [section 65(2)]

- An Interim CTO can last for any period up to 28 days. The Tribunal may grant more than one interim CTO. However, the total period may not exceed 56 consecutive days.
- An Interim CTO can authorise the same compulsory measures as a full CTO.
- If the patient is on a short-term detention certificate this is automatically revoked when an Interim CTO is made by the Tribunal.[34]

5. Tribunal Clerk must complete Form CTO 6 (Interim CTO)

- This is a seven-page form completed by the Tribunal Clerk who is present at the hearing and also later the hospital managers when they receive the form.
- The Tribunal records the source of the application; whether or not the Interim CTO has been granted and if so, which of the eight measures have been agreed and the length of the order, which must not exceed a period of 28 days.
- There is also a section on advance statements and to record where there is a conflict made by the patient under section 276(7)(a) of the Act.

6. Hospital Managers to admit patient to hospital/other place of residence if necessary [section 67(b)]

- If the person is not in hospital the section 67(1) CTO is a warrant that can be used to remove a person into hospital or another place of residence, if stated as one of the CTO measures in section 66(1). The authority to remove them can last for seven days.
- If the patient does not allow access to their home to exercise this removal, an authorised person, for example, a nurse, would then have to apply to the local sheriff court or justice of the peace for an "*entry to premises*" warrant under section 292[35] (see Chapter 6 on warrants).

7. Hospital Managers must appoint an RMO [section 230 (1)]

- This may already be the case if the AMP completing one of the Mental Health Reports has already been appointed as the RMO.[36]
- If the measures are a community-based interim CTO, the hospital managers still have to appoint an RMO who will oversee the medical treatment. The RMO, or another Psychiatrist appointed as a delegated RMO under section 230(3), is the only person who can review the order and/or apply to the Tribunal for a variation, regardless of where the patient is.[37]

8. Hospital Managers must complete Form CTO 1a (Record of Admission) and notify the Mental Welfare Commission

- The hospital managers must complete a Record of Admission and record the date when the Mental Welfare Commission was notified.

9. The Tribunal will review the Interim CTO and consider the (original) CTO application [section 64(4)]

- Before the Interim CTO expires, the original CTO application has to be considered by the Tribunal who have the same options as before, for example:

  i) grant the full CTO [section 64(4)(i)];
  ii) grant another Interim CTO (a total maximum of 56 days for all interim CTOs) [section 65(2)];
  iii) refuse the application [section 64(4)(b)].

10. The Tribunal must complete Form CTO 1, Part 5

- Part 5 – A compulsory treatment order

This is a record of the measures agreed by the Tribunal to make up the CTO. It lasts for six months and is completed by the Tribunal Clerk at the hearing itself. It includes the following details:

i) List of people who gave evidence.
ii) Formal decision whether or not the order was granted. All the conditions for a CTO under section 64(5) have to be met. It lists the measures that can be compelled for six months.
iii) List of recorded matters, that is, matters marked out as being essential to the care package.[38]
iv) Record of any conflict with the patient's advance statement and who this has been sent to.[39]

11. Hospital Managers have to receive the Tribunal's determination Form CTO 1, Part 5

- The Tribunal Clerk recording the options listed above will send a copy of the Form CTO 1, Part 5 to the Hospital Managers.

12. The CTO application is refused [section 64(4)(b)]

- If the application is refused, any current orders are immediately revoked by the RMO if they have not already expired. The patient can be discharged or remain in the hospital voluntarily as an informal patient.
- The Code of Practice suggests if the application is refused by the Tribunal, "*the RMO should oversee the drawing up and implementing of a full discharge plan of care.*"[40]
- The RMO/MHO or allocated social worker may choose to arrange a Care Programme Approach meeting with the consent of the patient to discuss a discharge care plan.

13. Hospital Managers to admit patient if necessary [section 67]

See heading **6.** above.

14. Hospital Managers to appoint an RMO [section 230(1)]

- This may already be the case if the AMP completing one of the Mental Health Reports has already been appointed as the RMO.[41]
- If the measures are a community-based CTO, the hospital managers have still to appoint an RMO who will oversee the medical treatment. The RMO, or delegated RMO under section 230(3), is the only person who can review the order and/or apply to the Tribunal for a variation, regardless of where the patient is.[42]

15. Hospital Managers complete Form CTO 1a and notify the Mental Welfare Commission

- The hospital managers must complete a Record of Admission and record the date when the Mental Welfare Commission was notified.
- The Hospital Managers have to send appropriate reading material to the patient with a copy to their named person about the following "*relevant matters*" relating to the detention:

  i) the provision in the Act whereby the patient is detained;
  ii) the consequences of the operation of that provision;
  iii) the powers of the RMO and the Tribunal in relation to revoking the order;
  iv) appeal rights, if applicable;
  v) the power of the Tribunal in dealing with these rights;
  vi) how the patient may exercise that right;
  vii) the functions of the Mental Welfare Commission in that order;
  viii) how the patient may obtain legal assistance to exercise that right.

Footnotes:

1 section 36(12); CoP, vol 2, chapter 7, para 48, p. 196.
2 section 36(8) (b)(ii).
3 CoP, vol 2, chapter 7. para 49, p. 197.
4 section 36(7).
5 CoP, vol 2 , chapter 7, para 61, p. 200.
6 section 39 – revoking the certificate because the criteria no longer met.
7 section 38(2) – AMP examines patient and is satisfied the criteria are still met up to 72 hours.
8 section 41(1) – patient's detention is suspended for any period within the 72 hour detention. Patient can leave hospital.
9 section 44(1) – patient detained for up to 28 days starting immediately after the short-term detention certificate is signed, that is, after MHO gives consent.
10 section 38(4).
11 Note: This also includes the patient although not listed under section 38(4). The hospital managers have a separate duty to provide information to any detained patients under the Act. The list of detentions include emergency certificates. [section 260(1)(a)(i)]. Provision times are stated in regulations. Scottish Statutory Instruments 2005/No.206. This is available under the website www.opsi.gov.uk
12 section 38(5)(b).
13 section 303(4)(b), that is, if the patient absconds for the remaining of the detention period.
14 section 55.

15 Form DET 2, Part 2. The best way to calculate the expiry is day 1 + 27 days. The first day is always included regardless of the time when the patient was detained.
16 section 44(6).
17 CoP, vol.2. chapter 2, para 63, p. 39 .
18 Note: This Form will not be passed onto a tribunal hearing if the patient does progress to a compulsory treatment order application.
19 section 230(1) ; CoP, vol 1, chapter 9, para 03, p. 133.
20 section 230(3); CoP op cit above.
21 Note: Only the patient's RMO can review a short-term certificate. This authority can be delegated to another AMP at any time under section 230(3)(b), for example, the Specialist Registrar.
22 Tribunal Rule 44 allows the Convener, either alone or with panel members, to dismiss an application. There are three basic reasons available as follows: 1. (i) outwith the jurisdiction of the Tribunal; (ii) made otherwise than in accordance with these Rules and has no reasonable prospect of success; or (iii) frivolous or vexatious. The Convener has the discretion to allow any relevant persons to be heard before making a final decision. [Tribunal Rule 44(4)].
23 Tribunal Rule 70 & 71; CoP, vol 2, chapter 3, para 81, p. 86.
24 Tribunal Rules: Rule 58. It is unlikely a Convener would hold a paper hearing for a CTO.
25 section 65(1), that is, the MHO has lodged a CTO application under section 63 for this right to apply.
26 See endnote (G), chapter 3 for discussion on possible reasons for an MHO requesting an interim CTO.
27 section 69(a).
28 Note: for further guidance see CoP, vol 2. Chapter 3, para 94, p.92.
29 section 65(2). This could be any person, for example, a care provider who has concerns, say, about contractual agreements in the proposed care plan.
30 section 65(6)(b).
31 section 65(3).
32 If these timescale are abused, for example, the patient's defence is still asking for more time to prepare their evidence, it brings into question the legal test of "necessity" as opposed to convenience.
33 section 64 (3)(a) to(e) and (g) to (i) ; section 65(4)(b) & (c) p. 44.
34 section 70.
35 section 66(1) lists eight measures. The most likely use of a section 292 warrant would be for the hospital or a condition of residence measure in section 66(1)(a) &(e).
36 section 58(2)(a).
37 section 230 (3)(a).
38 section 64(4)(a)(ii).
39 section 276(8)(a); section 276(8)(b).
40 CoP, vol 2, chapter 3, para 86, p. 89.
41 section 58(2)(a).
42 section 230(4)(a).

Appendix 3

Summary questions/answers on main aspects of the Act

Introduction

This is a useful summary for the general reader as well as the MHO to use as a quick-guide through the major procedures in the Act. It is a simple "walk through" the key concepts in the book.[1] There will be repetition with the chapters but these questions/responses are briefer.

1) Emergency detention certificate – section 36 of the 2003 Act (see Chapter 2)

1. What is an emergency detention certificate?

- A 72-hour detention certificate to allow a patient to be assessed in any hospital on a compulsory basis.
- The legal mandate is section 36 of the Mental Health (Care and Treatment) (Scotland) Act 2003.
- It can be completed by any registered medical practitioner including Senior House Officers (SHOs).

2. What is the content of the certificate – legal test?

(1) A six-page form in two parts:
   (i) Part 1 – medical certificate.
   (ii) Part 2 – admission details completed by the hospital manager.

(2) Detention criteria in text-boxes 1-5 which covers the following legal tests in section 36(4) & (5) of the Act:

   i) mental disorder – SHO does not have to state what this is [text box 1].

ii) significant impairment to decide on voluntary treatment [text box 2].
iii) urgency to detain patient [text box 3].
iv) significant risk to health, safety, welfare of patient; or safety of any other person [text box 4].
v) undesirable delay, that is, why short-term certificate not pursued [text box 5].

Other issues:
a) alternatives to detention [text box 6].
b) MHO consultation [text box 7].

The legal test is based on the *likelihood* a patient fulfils the need for detention. A definite diagnosis is not required at this stage. They should instead focus on the presenting symptoms and past history, if known.

3. When must it be completed?

- The medical practitioner (medic) can take as long as they want to assess the patient. The timescales begin when they start writing the Form DET 1. They then have up to 24 hours to complete the form that included seeking MHO consent.
- There is a minimum time of 4 hours if the medic starts the form between 8pm and midnight the same day, that is, this then restricts the time to only 4 hours. For example, if the medic starts the form at 9pm it must be completed within 4 hours, that is, 01.00 the following day [section 36(12)].

4. Can the medical practitioner dispense with MHO consent?

- No – unless there is an urgent need to complete the certificate and an MHO is not immediately available. The medic has to explain this in the form – text box 7, page 4.
- The MHO can give consent by telephone if they have seen the patient 48 hours prior to consent. The MHO then has to visit the detained patient within, say, 12 hours, or arrange for another colleague to visit the patient.[2]

5. What are the MHO duties? [section 36(d)]

- The main duty is to assess whether or not the detention criteria is fulfilled. This involves interviewing the patient and discussion with the medical practitioner. The satisfaction test includes eliminating informal and less restrictive treatment approaches.[3]
- After giving consent, the MHO should detail in a report to the medical practitioner the reasons for giving or not giving consent.[4]
- The MHO has a specific duty to preserve patient's property; to consider the needs of dependent and pets.[5]

6. Who can revoke this certificate?[6]

- Only an approved Psychiatrist termed an "approved medical practitioner" [AMP] can revoke (or cancel) a certificate.[7]

7. What other review options are available?[8]

- The AMP has three other options as follows:
  (1) to complete a short-term certificate at any time within 72 hours.[9] This need not be after the first examination.
  (2) Suspend the detention for any period within the certificate, for example, to attend a funeral;[10]
  (3) to lapse the certificate and let it expire after 72 hours.

8. Can the patient appeal?

- The Patient has no right of appeal. They can only appeal if the legal process has not been observed correctly through a judicial review.

9. Where can I find the Form DET 1 and the legislation/ Code of Practice?

- The forms are published by the Mental Welfare Commission for Scotland and are available online at: www.mwcscot.org.uk (look under "New Forms" where they are listed)
- The 2003 Act: www.opsi.gov.uk

- Code of Practice: This is in 3 volumes. The relevant reference for this volume 2. Website: www.scotland.gov.uk/publications

2) Short-term detention certificate – section 44 of the 2003 Act (see Chapter 2)

1. What is a short-term detention certificate?

- A 28-day detention certificate to allow a patient to be assessed and treated in any type of hospital on a compulsory basis.
- The legal mandate is section 44(1) of the Act.
- It can only be completed by an approved medical practitioner.

2. What is the content of the certificate – legal test?

Form DET 2 is in two parts:

(i) Part 1 – the medical certificate.
(ii) Part 2 – notification by hospital managers.

- Detention criteria – in 5 text boxes which covers the following legal tests in section 44(4) of the Act:

    i) mental disorder – SHO does not have to state what this is [text box 1].
    ii) significant impairment to decide on voluntary treatment [text box 2].
    iii) necessary to detain patient to assess and give medical treatment [text box 3].
    iv) significant risk to health, safety, welfare of patient; or safety of any other person [text box 4].
    v) necessity – to grant the short-term certificate [text box 5].

- The legal test is based on the "*likelihood*" the patient fulfils the need for detention in section 44(3)(b). The AMP does not have to state what the mental disorder is. They should focus on the presenting symptoms and past history, if known.

3. When must it be completed?

- The AMP can take as long as they want to assess the patient. The timescales begin when they start writing the Form DET 2. They then have up to 72 hours to complete the form. This includes seeking MHO consent.[11]
- The Act allows an AMP to detain a person when either at home or in hospital using a short-term detention certificate. The timescale to complete this certificate would however be shortened if the patient is already in hospital and detained under an EDC [section 38(2)].
- When complete, the AMP then has 72 hours to admit the patient to any hospital.[12]
- If the patient is already in hospital either informally or detained under an EDC, the short-term detention period begins from midnight on the day the certificate was completed.[13] The emergency certificate is then revoked.

4. Can the medical practitioner dispense with MHO consent?

- No. There are no exceptions to this rule.
- The MHO can give consent without a formal interview in exceptional circumstances where there are communication difficulties that cannot be speedily overcome, for example, where the patient is extremely dangerous or violent; where the patient refuses to co-operate or participate in the interview. The Code of Practice emphasises the MHO should "*at the very least*" be in the presence of the person being detained.[14]
- The MHO can give consent by telephone but only in exceptional circumstances. The Code of Practice suggests this would apply where the MHO could not access the patient, for example, ferry strikes.[15]

5. What are the MHO duties?[16] [Section 45]

- The main duties are to interview the patient; identify the named person (if any); inform the patient of availability of independent advocacy services.
- If the MHO cannot perform some of these duties (more than likely

given normal practice), they have seven calendar days to seek out the information and inform the AMP.[17]

- The revised Form DET 2 from August 2007 in text box 6, however, now allows the MHO to give reasons why they were unable to perform all or some of the legal duties outlined above. The form advises "*by completing this there is no longer a requirement to complete Form DET 3.*" This is optional as the MHO may wish to pursue the issue of identifying and then vetting a named person. The MHO could also state in this text box their intention to write to independent advocacy services about the patient's admission.
- The MHO has to send letters to various people after giving consent.

Summary of letters as follows:

Letter 1	MHO to medical practitioner (GP, SHO, AMP) confirming consent/non-consent of emergency/short-term certificate.
Letter 2	MHO to named person reference appeal/advocacy rights for a short-term certificate.
Letter 3	MHO to patient reference appeal/advocacy rights for a short-term certificate.
Letter 4	MHO to Advocacy Services informing them of the section 44 certificate.

6. Who can revoke this certificate?

- Only a patient's RMO can revoke a certificate.[18] This can be done at any time.

7. What other review options are available?[19]

- The RMO has four other options as follows:

  (1) Suspend the detention for any period within the hospital grounds;[20]
  (2) To lapse the certificate and let it expire after 28 days.
  (3) To request that the MHO apply for a CTO.[21]

(4) To extend the certificate for a further three working days to allow the MHO to apply for a CTO.[22]

8. Can the patient/named person appeal? [section 50]

- Yes. They can appeal independently during any period of the detention.
- The RMO and MHO involved in the patient's current treatment would be formally invited by the Tribunal to attend the hearing and given the opportunity to answer the points of appeal.[23]
- The appeal may not be exclusively about the certificate. It could be any aspect of the assessment or treatment. The Tribunal do not usually give the reasons for the appeal when notifying the RMO/MHO. The assumption would be the patient is appealing against the certificate. The patient/named person is entitled to free legal aid regardless of income.

9. What is an extension short-term certificate? [section 47]

- A patient's RMO can extend a section 44 certificate for an additional 3 working days from the original 28-day certificate, excluding weekends and Scottish Bank holidays[24] to allow an MHO to apply to the Tribunal for a CTO. The RMO must have MHO consent.
- The reasons for this extension are two-fold – the original section 44 criteria apply and due to a change in the patient's mental health further detention is required. The RMO is not allowed to repeat the section 44 certificate.

10. Where can I find the Form DET 2 and the legislation/ Code of Practice?

- The forms are published by the Mental Welfare Commission for Scotland and available online at: www.mwcscot.org.uk (look under "New Act Forms" and they are all listed).
- The 2003 Act: type in "Scottish legislation"
- Code of Practice: this is in 3 volumes. The relevant reference for this is volume 2. Website: www.scotland.gov.uk/publications

3) Compulsory treatment order – section 64(4)(i) (see Chapter 3)

Details:

1. What is a compulsory treatment order?

- Initially a 6-month civil compulsory order to allow a patient to be assessed and treated either in a specific hospital or elsewhere in the community.
- The legal mandate is section 66(1) of the Act.
- The CTO can only be granted by a tribunal hearing made up of three members – legal/medical/general. The legal member chairs the Tribunal and is termed the Convener.
- Only an MHO can apply to the Tribunal for a CTO. The application pack is called FORM CTO 1 and is composite, that is, in five parts as follows:

Part 1	Patient/MHO details/notifications.
Part 2	MHO report under section 61(2).
Part 3	Proposed Care Plan under section 62.
Part 4	Application for a compulsory treatment order.
Part 5	The CTO itself completed by the tribunal hearing.

- The MHO has to submit this (composite) application pack along with two mental health reports prepared by the patient's RMO and/or another AMP/patient's GP. The GP should only complete the report if they know the patient. It should be an independent report and not be influenced by the RMO's report.
- Both mental health reports have to agree on the measures sought and also at least one of the three possible types of mental disorder, that is, mental illness/personality disorder/learning disability listed under section 328.
- There are eight measures available to the Tribunal within any CTO as follows:

i) hospital detention;
ii) treatment (either in hospital/community);
iii) attendance requirement for medical treatment;
iv) attendance requirement for community care services;
v) residential requirement;
vi) access requirement for MHO/RMO and relevant others;
vii) MHO approval to change address;
viii) Patient to notify MHO when address is changed.

- The Tribunal can only grant measures i) ii) & ii) to viii) separately, that is, hospital and community-based CTOs cannot be granted at the same time.
- The Tribunal can grant an Interim CTO for up to 28 days at a time to allow for more evidence.
- The legal test is the same as for a CTO (see **2.** below).
- Interim CTOs under section 65 are very common given the short timescale for submission.

2. What is the content of the certificate – legal test? [section 64(5)]

- The evidence for the CTO is recorded in the text boxes of the mental health reports that cover the following legal tests in section 64(5) of the Act.

  i) mental disorder – medic has to describe the symptoms but does not necessarily have to state the diagnosis [text box 2].
  ii) availability of medical treatment which is likely to prevent the mental disorder worsening or alleviate any of the symptoms, or effect, of the disorder.
  iii) significant risk to patient's health, safety or welfare or to the safety of any other person.
  iv) significant impairment to decide on voluntary treatment.
  v) necessity – the CTO has a purpose according to medic's satisfaction.

- The legal test for the tribunal hearing is they are "*satisfied*" those five criteria have been met.
- This therefore leaves the assessment of evidence open-ended.[25]

3. When must the CTO application be completed?

- The MHO has 14 calendar days to submit the CTO application pack to the Tribunal after the second mental health report has been completed. The mental health reports have to be completed within five calendar days.
- If the patient is already detained under a short-term detention certificate (28 days) or an extended short-term detention certificate (3 working days), the MHO has to submit the application pack before they expire. The law allows this application to be submitted even on the last day of the certificate but best practice would suggest this process begin around the middle of the patient's current detention.[26]
- There is a sample CTO application pack in the MHO Training Pack.

4. What are the other main MHO duties? [section 60]

- The main duties are to interview the patient; inform them of appeal rights/independent advocacy services. The MHO also has to identify a named person and inform them of their appeal rights.
- The MHO has an additional duty to assess the suitability of the named person. If the MHO thinks the named person is unsuitable, he has a statutory duty to apply to the Tribunal to have them replaced. This applies to nominated and default named persons.[27]
- If the (suitable) named person does not wish to take part in the Tribunal proceedings, the MHO can prepare a standard letter for the named person to sign, waiving their rights of appeal/notification/consultation.
- The standard notification letters are as follows:[28]

> **Letter 1: section 61(2)(a)-(d)**
> MHO to patient informing them of their rights/availability of advocacy services/informing patient the application is being made.

Letter 2: section 60(1)(b)
MHO to named person informing them of the CTO application.

Letter 3
MHO letter to the Mental Welfare Commission reference CTO application under section 60(1)(c).

Letter 4: section 60(2)(c)(ii)
MHO to independent advocacy services about the CTO application.

5. What if the patient cannot instruct a solicitor?

- The RMO has to record on the mental health report whether or not a patient has the capacity to instruct a solicitor.
- If not, the Tribunal can arrange a "Person of skill" (usually a solicitor) to visit the patient and confirm this before the first hearing.[29]
- The next stage is for the hearing to appoint a Curator *ad litem* to act on the patient's behalf throughout all the hearings. The Curator can then commission an independent medical opinion to oppose the application.
- If the patient has capacity, their legal representative can commission an independent medical opinion.

6. Can the MHO have legal representation?

- Yes. This should be available from the MHO's Legal Services department.
- The Tribunal rules allow for the MHO to have any person assisting them at the Tribunal, for example, another experienced MHO.
- The MHO should have stated in Part 1 of the CTO application pack who they wish to attend to give evidence. This would normally be the patient's RMO/named nurse/care provider if it were a community-based CTO.
- The MHO should ensure copies of the CTO application pack plus the two mental health reports are lodged with Legal Services in good time before the hearing is arranged.

7. What if the MHO/RMO is unavailable? [section 229(2) for MHOs/section 230(3) for RMOs]

- The Act allows for the MHO/RMO to delegate responsibility in this event using section 229(2) and section 230(3) respectively.
- Only an MHO and an RMO can be delegated. This does not extend to other social work colleagues or junior grade doctors.[30]

8. How long does the CTO last? [section 64(4)(i)]

- A CTO granted by a Tribunal is for six months.
- The patient's RMO can extend the CTO for another six months and then for a year with the consent of an MHO.
- If the MHO does not consent to these extensions, a tribunal hearing has to be convened.[31]
- The Tribunal have to arrange a hearing if the CTO lasts for more than two years.
- This has still to be rolled out across Scotland. It started in 2007.

9. Where can I find the Form CTO 1 and the legislation/ Code of Practice?

- The forms are published by the Mental Welfare Commission for Scotland and available online at: www.mwcscot.org.uk (look under "New Act Forms" and they are listed).
- The 2003 Act: website: type "Scottish legislation".
- Code of Practice: This is in 3 volumes. The relevant reference for this volume is 2. Website: www.scotland.gov.uk/publications

4) Social circumstances reports [section 231] (see Chapter 8)

1. Introduction

MHOs are used to writing SCR's. With the 1984 Act they were classified as statutory and non-statutory. The latter were optional if the MHO gave consent to the detention. The Scottish councils operated different policies.
The Act now makes SCR's statutory. They have to be completed after a "*relevant event*" which includes practically all the civil and criminal detentions. These nine events are listed in section 232 as follows:

1. Short-term detention certificate [section 44(1)].
2. Interim compulsory treatment order [section 65(2)].
3. Compulsory treatment order [section 64(4)].
4. Assessment order [section 130 ss.52D (2)].
5. Treatment order [section 130 ss. 52M(2)].
6. Interim compulsion order [section 131 ss. 53(2)].
7. Compulsion order [section 133 ss.57A(2)].
8. Hospital direction [section 59A CPA 1995].
9. Transfer for treatment direction [section 136(2)].

The only exception is the 3-day emergency certificate.

One concession is MHOs do not have to prepare an SCR if they consider it would serve little or no practical purpose.[32] This is a judgement issue. Reasons could be as follows:

1. An SCR has just been completed, for example, a short-term detention certificate and therefore there is no need to complete an SCR for an interim CTO or a CTO.
2. The short-term certificate period did not last the full 28-day period and a CTO application was not pursued.

The Form SCR 1 is made up of the following sections:

1. Patient details
2. MHO details
3. Requirement for an SCR.

- The requirement for an SCR allows the MHO to decide whether or not an SCR is necessary and to state those reasons in text box 1.
- As with the 1984 Act the MHO has to complete the SCR within 21 days of the relevant event and send a copy to the patient's RMO and the Mental Welfare Commission.

2. Plan of social circumstances report

1) The Act prescribes the information required in an SCR. This is outlined in the regulations.[33] The headings are also summarised in the SCR form itself. Best practice would suggest the MHO follow these headings to the letter.
   This style of SCR preparation using the statutory headings can also be transferred to the personal circumstances part of the CTO application form in text box 3 where the MHO has discretion based on relevance to include or add further information.

2) The MHO may wish to make it clear at the top of the SCR form the source of their headings, that is, the regulation reference.

Note: The MHO might find writing the SCR to be impersonal and almost programmatic. Given SCR preparation is now a statutory duty under regulations it invites this particular style. Note that each of the statutory headings is used in the narrative of the form. It makes reading easier to follow.

Legal references:

Source: i) Mental Health (Care and Treatment) (Scotland) Act 2003.

ii) Scottish Statutory Instrument 2005 No. 310 –
The Mental Health (social circumstances reports) (Scotland) Regulations 2005. Website: "scottish legislation"

iii) Code of Practice, volume 1, chapter 11, paras 01 to 17, pp. 160-166
Website: www.scotland.gov.uk under "Publications"

3. Application of SCR to legislation – MHO duties [section 231]

Details:

1) legal references to MHO duties:

i) Section 231(1)
SCR to be prepared within 21 days from day one of a relevant event.
Copy to RMO/Commission.

ii) Section 231(2)
exemption from preparing SCR – "*serve little, or no, practical purpose*"; record the reasons and send this statement to the RMO/Commission.

iii) Section 231(3)
regulations quoted above which prescribes what information is to be included in the SCR.

iv) Section 232
outlines the list of civil/criminal orders where an SCR is required.

2) Regulations: The Mental Health (social circumstances report) Regulation 2005 No. 310

This is the 'bible' for MHOs doing SCR's. There are 19 headings lettered (a) to (s) which the MHO should use. As discussed above, the MHO may wish to include the headings within the SCR.

3) Code of Practice volume 1, Chapter 11, paragraphs 01-17, pages 160-166.

This is a thorough discussion of the details and thinking behind the SCR. It has six headings as follows:

i) Overview of the statutory provisions [paras 01-04].
ii) What is the purpose of an SCR [para 05].
iii) Whom should the MHO interview and/or consult in preparing an SCR [paras 07-11].
iv) In what circumstances might preparing an SCR *"serve little, or no, practical purpose"* [paras 12-15].
v) What is the difference between an SCR, a proposed care plan and a MHO's report which both accompany the application for a compulsory treatment order[34] [paras 16-17].
vi) Can an MHO trainee prepare an SCR [para 19].

5) Reviews. Part 7 of the 2003 Act (see Chapter 4)

1. What are reviews?

- They are a means of re-assessing whether or not a person detained under civil or criminal compulsory order still requires detention.
- All reviews must be done by a detained patient's RMO or delegated to another AMP.

2. What are the choices for an RMO in a review?

- An RMO can do one of the following:
  i) Revoke the order – at any time.
  ii) Extend the order by another 6 or 12 months – it can only be extended within the last two months of the existing order.
  iii) Vary the order – it can only be varied within the first four or eight months of the order depending on the length of the order, that is, 6 or 12 months.
  iv) Extend and vary the order – within the last two months of the existing order.
- The RMO can extend an order for up to 2 years on their own provided they have agreement from an MHO. This is called a "*section 86 determination*". If the MHO disagrees with this extension, then a tribunal hearing has to be heard.[35]

- Other types of reviews can only be decided by a Tribunal, that is, vary/extend and vary.[36]

3. When must the reviews be done? [section 77, 78, 80]

- The RMO has a statutory duty to do reviews within 2 months of the expiry of any order. These are called "*mandatory reviews*". The first mandatory review can only extend the order by 6 months; further mandatory reviews can extend by 12 months.
- The RMO can review the order on an informal basis within the mandatory review periods. This is called a "*from time to time*" review. The choices are then limited to revoking the order or varying the order. Extending it within the first 4-month period would affect the patient's human rights. Only the mandatory reviews allow the RMO to extend the orders as they apply at the end of the order (see immediately above).

4. In what way is the MHO involved in reviews?

- The MHO has to be consulted for the mandatory reviews. The MHO has to state whether they agree or disagree with the RMO's proposal to extend/extend and vary an order.
- If the MHO disagrees with extending the orders only then a tribunal hearing has to be held.
- The MHO has a right to be heard at tribunal hearings for other forms of reviews, that is, vary/extend and vary.
- The RMO has to seek a vew of agreement/disagreement from an MHO in from *"time to time"* reviews where he wishes to vary the order.[37]
- A Tribunal must be held if a patient's order is more than 2 years old and has not been formally reviewed by a Tribunal.[38]

5. What are the MHO duties? [section 85 & section 89]

- The MHO's duties relate to the first and further mandatory reviews where the RMO wishes to either extend/extend and vary an order. The duties for both types are similar as follows:

i) interview the patient and inform them of their legal /advocacy rights.
ii) take appropriate steps to ensure the patient has access to a solicitor and independent advocacy services.
iii) inform the RMO whether or not they agree with the review proposals.

- The MHO has no formal role to inform the patient's named person of the review. This is left for the RMO to do before they send their proposal to extend/extend and vary an order.[39]
- The Tribunal has discretion under section 109(2) to require the MHO to prepare a report to assist the Tribunal in making a decision where an order is being varied; extended; extended and varied.[40] These headings are as follows:

(a) on the steps that the Mental Health Officer has taken to comply with the requirements imposed by section 85(2); 89(2) (MHO's duties to patient, and so on);
(b) giving the views of the Mental Health Officer on the application and the reasons for those views;
(c) giving, if known to the Mental Health Officer, the views of the patient and the patient's named person on the application and the reasons for those views;
(d) giving, in so far as the Mental Health Officer considers purposes of the application, details of the personal circumstances of the patient;
(e) giving, if known to the Mental Health Officer, details of any advance statement that the patient has made (and not withdrawn); and
(f) giving any other information which the Mental Health Officer considers may assist the Tribunal in considering the application.

- The Scottish Executive have stated the MHO need not supply a report unless so required by the Tribunal under their ancillary powers in section 109(2).
- Given the key role the MHO has in the reviews, best practice would suggest these headings be used as a guide to summarising

consultations.

- There are suggested template letters the MHO could use in their duties under section 85 and section 89 as follows:

Letter 1:	MHO to patient and named person[41] informing him of the RMO's proposal; rights of appeal; availability of independent advocacy.
Letter 2:	MHO to RMO reference agreement/disagreement with the proposal – adapted according to the type of review.
Letter 3:	MHO to Independent Advocacy Service reference review.

6. Can the patient/named person appeal their Order? [Section 99 & 100]

- Yes. They can both appeal separately at specific periods in the order. The restrictions for patient/named person appeals are as follows:

  i) The original CTO/extended CTO by the Tribunal under section 102/extended and varied CTO by the Tribunal under section 103(1) has to run for at least 3 months before an appeal is allowed.
  ii) If they lose the appeal to revoke or vary the CTO, they are allowed one further application for the duration of the order, that is, within either the initial 6 months of the CTO; the extended 6 months or the next 12-month period.

- The same restrictions also apply where the RMO extends the CTO and the patient/named person appeals this under section 99 , that is, only one further appeal is allowed within the period of extension.
- The AMP and MHO involved would then be formally invited by the Tribunal to attend the hearing and be given the opportunity to answer the points of appeal.
- The Tribunal have ancillary powers under section 109(2) to request an MHO report (see **5.** above).

- The appeal may not be exclusively about the order. It could be any aspect of the assessment or treatment. The Tribunal do not usually give the reasons for the appeal when notifying the AMP/MHO. The assumption would be the patient is appealing against the order.
- The patient/named person is entitled to free legal aid regardless of their income.

7. What are the patient/named person rights in reviews? [section 103(5)]

- If a Tribunal is held, that is, to extend/vary/extend and vary a CTO, they have a right to be heard at a Tribunal and have legal representation. This is not the same as a patient appeal as the applicant is the patient's RMO. The patient also has a right to independent advocacy services. The MHO has to inform the patient (only) of these rights (see **5.** above)

8. Where can I find further information on reviews: legislation/Code of Practice?

- The 2003 Act: Part 7; Chapter 4 Review of Orders.
  Website:
  www.opsi.gov.uk/scotlegislation/acts_scotparliament.htm
- Code of Practice: This is in 3 volumes. The relevant reference for this is volume 2; chapter 5, pages 119-165.
  Website: www.scotland.gov.uk/publications

6) Warrants [section 35 & 293] (see Chapter 6)

1. What is a warrant/order?

- This is a means to enter a person's home by force if necessary to assess and, if where applicable, remove that person to a place of safety. There are warrants for:
  - i) assessment within a person's home and
  - ii) a separate order to remove a person to be assessed/ treated elsewhere, for example, a hospital.

    - i) Section 35 – three separate warrants
      - a) enter premises;
      - b) allow a medical practitioner to examine the person for up to 3 hours;
      - c) allow a medical practitioner to access the person's medical records without their consent.
    - ii) Section 293 – removal order – remove a person who has been formally diagnosed as having a mental disorder to a place of safety for up to 7 days.

2. Why is an MHO involved in warrants?

- The MHO is the only person who can apply for a warrant. This is the same for CTO applications.

3. What are the criteria for each warrant?

i) Section 33(1) – the person:
  - a) appears to have a mental disorder and
  - b) appears to be exposed to ill-treatment/neglect or receiving some other deficiency in care or treatment at some place other than a hospital;
  - c) has property that is damaged or is likely to be damaged;
  - d) is living alone or without care and unable to look after himself or his property or financial affairs;

e) and the safety of some other person may be at risk.

ii) Section 293 – removal order
The person has a mental disorder and a) to d) as above. The only difference is the person has to be diagnosed as having a mental disorder.

4. How does the MHO obtain a warrant?

i) Section 35 – enter premises/medical exam/access to records.
The MHO can apply to either the local sheriff court or a justice of the peace through the District Court to grant the warrant.[42] There are prescribed forms on the Mental Welfare Commission website.
The MHO should contact the court or Legal Services in the first instance for advice to access a sheriff/JP.

ii) Section 293 – removal order
The MHO should always try to seek a sheriff to sign the warrant. The only exception to use a justice of the peace is urgency.[43]

5. What are the timescales to implement the warrants?

i) Section 35
8 days expiry after warrant is granted.[44]

ii) Section 293
72 hours to use the warrant after granted; 7 days to hold the person in a place of safety.[45]

6. Can the patient appeal?

i) Section 35
No right of appeal.

ii) Section 293
The subject of the order has a right to be heard before the removal order is granted by a sheriff but not with a justice of the peace.[46]

They can later apply to the court to have the order recalled or varied.[47]

7. Does the MHO have to notify anyone after the warrant is implemented? [section 35(10)]

- Yes – but only for a section 35 warrant. The MHO has to notify the Mental Welfare Commission "*as to whether a warrant was granted or refused.*"

8. Summary practice points

i) Police Constable does not have to be named.
They will act on the warrant/order.

ii) If the MHO plans to take any professionals with them to enter the premises then the MHO has to specify in the warrant who they are, for example, CPN/medic.
   (a) Form MHO1 – MHO application;
   (b) Form MHO1A – warrant signed by Sheriff/JP.

iii) Warrant allowing person to be detained in their home for up to 3 hours for a medical examination. This can be done by any rank of doctor as long as they are registered medical practitioners.
   (a) Form MH02 – MHO application;
   (b) Form MH02A – warrant signed by a sheriff or a justice of the peace.

iv) The MHO cannot use the warrant to remove the person. The options are a section 36/44 detention certificate which can then effect a removal or using a removal order.
The removal order is however time-limited, that is, up to 7 days. The MHO would need to specify in the application the purpose of a removal order and also the exact amount of days required as the Act describes the removal period as *"not exceeding 7 days, as may be specified in the order"* [section 293(3)(c)(ii).

v) If detained under section 36 & 44, this certificate would last for 72 hours, thus giving adequate time to transfer the patient to hospital.

vi) The duty to inquire is a local authority function and not for the MHO. The MHO is involved only if access is denied. The legal test is "*appear*" under section 33 (1). Other agencies are also obliged to co-operate under section 34 with the Local Authority in this inquiry.

vii) The MHO should look at the grounds for inquiry under section 33 and then select the ones to be used as evidence in the section 35 application. The MHO should also consider taking the professionals involved to present their evidence before a court or a signing JP. The MHO role as applicant is to lead the evidence using relevant witnesses.

9. Where can I find further information on warrants: legislation/Code of Practice?

- The 2003 Act: Part 4; Chapter 2 Review of Orders.
  Website: www.oqps.gov.uk/scotlegislation/acts_scotparliament.htm
- Code of Practice.
  This is in 3 volumes. The relevant reference is volume 1, chapter 15, pp. 203-229.
  Website: www.scotland.gov.uk/publications.

7) Named person [section 250 to section 181] (see Chapter 7)

1. What is a named person?

- This is anyone over the age of 16 living in the UK, Channel Islands or the Isle of Man who has been nominated by a Scottish-based person ["*nominator*"] to act on their behalf in the event of being subject to the Act [section 254(6)(c)].
- The person nominated is not obliged to accept the nomination and can give notice of this to the nominator and the Scottish local authority where the nominator lives (see **2(b)** below).
- The nominator can do this at any time regardless of whether they are mentally ill or not. This is similar to making a power of attorney, only this time the focus is on mental disorder.
- The legal test for capacity to nominate derives from the Adults with Incapacity (Scotland) Act 2000. The nomination excludes any person who has incapacity due to a mental disorder or inability to communicate.
- Only one person can be nominated at any time. Named persons do not include groups or professionals involved with the nominator, for example, MHO, CPN, GP and so forth. They would have a conflict of interest.

2(a) How is a named person nominated? [section 250; section 251]

Nomination is done in two ways as follows:

i) Formal nomination: [section 250]
A person can be nominated in writing. This requires a "*prescribed person*" to ensure the person making the nomination understands the effect of the nomination and is not under any undue pressure to make this nomination.
There are template forms issued by the Mental Welfare Commission for this purpose but this can be done by any means.
The prescribed person is chosen by regulations. They include social

workers; occupational therapists; registered nurses, medical practitioners; solicitors; anyone employed in the provision of a care service.[48]

ii) Default nomination: [section 251]
This arises after a person is subject to the Act and there is no nominated named person. The default is firstly to the (unpaid) primary carer who provides a substantial amount of care on a regular basis. The next order is the patient's nearest relative. The order of default nomination is listed in section 254 under "*meaning of nearest relative*". The first is the patient's spouse; next comes partnership (including same sex) who have been living together for more than six months.[49]

2(b) Can a named person decline the nomination?

Section 250(6) – nomination declined by person.
Section 251(6) – person nominated declined by primary carer.
Section 254(5) – person nominated declined by nearest relative.

- Yes. The named person – whether through a nomination or by default – can decline the nomination at any time.
- The Act requires withdrawal to be in writing to the local authority where the nominator lives and also a copy to the relevant person making the nomination.
- If the named person refuses to make a formal statement but at the same time makes it clear they do not wish to be the named person, the MHO can record this and send this record to their local authority; the Tribunal and the Mental Welfare Commission.[50]

Note: See template letter in Chapter 9 under "*named person*" for this purpose. This is addressed to the MHO given they have the sole legal responsibility for identifying a named person.

2(c) Can a named person decline their involvement at a tribunal hearing?

- Yes. The Tribunal Rules allow for the named person to waive their rights to receive notification of hearings; also to waive any right of appeal where a Tribunal is obliged to consult them before granting an order that is different from the original application.[51]
- This does not mean the named person role is no longer valid. It is just an opportunity for the named person to absent themselves from the hearing. They do not have to give reasons. Furthermore, the MHO should not feel pressurised at the tribunal hearing to give reasons. It may be, for example, that the named person is ill or attendance would make relations with the patient worse. The named person's legal powers remain for other aspects of the patient's detention, for example, consultation with the RMO.
- If the named person is unable to write to the Tribunal, the MHO can do so in their place under section 255(5) but stating the named person does not wish to fulfil that part of their role.

Note: There is a template letter in Chapter 9 for a named person to use as a means of waiving their notification and/or appeal rights. This is addressed to the Convener at the Tribunal.

3. What is the role of the MHO in identifying a named person? [section 255]

- The MHO has an exclusive legal role in identifying a named person regardless of the type of nomination.
- Section 255 gives detailed requirements on what an MHO shall/may do when a person is subject to the Act as follows:

  i) establish who the named person is – if nominated/default [section 255 (2)].
  ii) where the person does not have a named person or is unable to establish whether or not the patient has a named person, the MHO has discretion whether or not to apply to the Tribunal to have a named person nominated by the Tribunal [section 255(4)(b)].

iii) where the patient has a named person but the MHO considers that named person to be inappropriate, the MHO has to apply to the Tribunal to remove that (apparent) named person from the role and where possible, replace them with another named person recommended by the MHO [section 255 (6)].

Note: The compulsory element for the MHO to apply to the Tribunal arises where the MHO has a specific duty to identify a named person, for example, section 44 short-term certificate [section 45 (1)(b)]; CTO applications [section 59]; compulsion orders [section 138].

iv) When the MHO comes across a situation where there is no named person, they have discretion as to whether or not to apply to the Tribunal for a replacement. The Act describes this as where the MHO is "*discharging any function*". CTO reviews are a good example.[52]

4. Can a person prevent someone they know from being a named person? [section 253]

- A person who has either made a nomination or not, can make a formal written declaration against another person being appointed as a named person.
- A prescribed person must witness this in writing in the same way as a nomination (see **2.(a)(i)** above).

Note: The Tribunal is not bound by the terms of a declaration so can disregard them. They may do so where the MHO still supports the original nomination and can give an opinion to the Tribunal why the reasons for the declaration were not valid, for example, a caring mother who is supporting the application. Equally, the MHO could support the patient's declaration especially if they were not originally involved as the prescribed person.

5. Who is a child's named person? [section 252]

- This would normally be their parent, usually the eldest or, if disputed, the MHO decides.
- If the child is "*looked after*" under section 31 of the Children Act 1989, the local authority is the named person until they cease to be looked after.
- In any other case, a primary carer who is over the age of 16, for example, a grandparent.

6. Does a patient always have a named person?

- No. This applies as follows:
  - i) Where the person has made a declaration about person(s) they do not want to be the named person. This can be done as a group, for example, stated family members.
  - ii) Where a named person declines the nomination and the MHO cannot find a suitable replacement.
  - iii) Where the MHO assesses a named person as inappropriate and does not have a replacement.

- The important issue is for the MHO to demonstrate they have taken reasonable steps to identify a named person. The MHO has also to record their efforts and send a copy to the Tribunal and the Mental Welfare Commission.[53]

7. Where can I find further information on named person legislation/Code of Practice?

- The 2003 Act: Part 17; Chapter 1, named person.
  Website: type "scottish legislation"
- Code of Practice: This is in 3 volumes. The relevant reference for this is volume 1; Chapter 6, pages 82-93.
  Website: www.scotland.gov.uk/publications
- The nomination/declaration forms /guide to named persons are on the Mental Welfare Commission website:
  www.mwcscot.org.uk under "Publications".

Footnotes:

1 Note: criminal proceedings are omitted as Chapter 5 itself adopts a similar style.
2 CoP, vol 2, chapter 7, para 43, p. 195. This would exclude out-of-hours MHOs giving telephone consent.
3 CoP, vol 2, chapter 7, paras 39-42, pp. 193-194.
4 CoP, vol 2, chapter 7, para 45, p. 193. See Chapter 9, under 2) Letter 1.
5 CoP, vol 2, chapter 7, para 57, p. 198. This refers to the National Assistance Act 1948.
6 Section 39.
7 An AMP is someone who has been formally tested as having special experience in the diagnosis and treatment of mental disorder. This is stated in section 22 of the Act. AMP's are usually drawn from the Consultant grade but they can also be associate specialists or staff grade specialists with appropriate seniority. They undergo a two-tier test organised through the four Scottish medical deaneries.
8 Note. Section 38(2) allows an AMP up to 72 hours to consider these options.
9 section 44(1).
10 section 41(1).
11 section 44(3)(d).
12 section 44(5)(a).
13 section 44(5)(b)(ii).
14 CoP, vol 2, chapter 2, para 42, p. 32.
15 CoP, vol 2, chapter 2, para 44, p. 33.
16 CoP, vol 2, chapter 2, paras 34-40, pp. 30-32 .
17 section 45(2).
18 section 230: After being detained under a short-term certificate, the hospital managers have to appoint a responsible medical officer. They are AMPs but change their legal role to be responsible for that patient's care throughout the period of detention. The RMO, and not an AMP, can suspend or revoke a short-term certificate. Any AMP however can extend a short-term certificate, presumably owing to the emergency nature of the medical circumstances.
19 Note: The Act allows the RMO up to 28 days to consider these options.
20 section 53(1) – this can be for hours or days within the duration of the certificate period. A suspension certificate has to be completed any time a detained patient leaves the hospital grounds. It can only be completed by the patient's RMO.
21 section 57(1).
22 section 47(1). This would be where the detained patient's mental health has deteriorated. The RMO must have MHO approval and also apply to the Tribunal themselves using Form DET 4.
23 section 50(3)(e) & (f).
24 Scottish Bank holidays differ from local authority public holidays which vary across Scotland. There are eight statutory Bank holidays/annum. The Act only recognises Bank holidays.
25 section 64(4)(a). Each tribunal hearing is autonomous. Their decisions can only be appealed through the court system under section 320(1)(b).
26 Note: It may be the MHO has insufficient time to prepare parts of the CTO application pack due to the lateness of mental health reports. If this is the case, the MHO should consider requesting an interim CTO under section 65(2). In any case, the Tribunal are legally obliged under section 69(a) to consider the need for an interim where a person is detained either under a short-term or an extension short-term certificate before going on to look at a CTO application.
27 section 255(6).

28 See Chapter 9 for these template letters.
29 This system is currently being revised where a Curator *ad litem* can be appointed immediately if the MHO informs the Tribunal headquarters before the initial hearing.
30 section 229(2) – MHO; section 230(3) – RMO.
31 section 101(2)(b). This section applied to restricted patients detained under criminal proceedings from October 2006. It has been delayed for civil and other criminal proceedings orders to October 2007.
32 section 231(2).
33 Scottish Statutory Instruments 2005/No. 310.
34 Form CTO 1 has a section in Part 2 [MHO report] termed "details of personal circumstances of the patient".
35 section 101(2)(a)(ii) .
36 section 103.
37 section 93(4)(c) amended by Scottish Statutory Instrument 2004/No.533.
38 section 101(2)(b). See footnote 31 above.
39 section 87(2)(c)(ii); section 91(b).
40 Scottish Statutory Instrument 2005; No. 366, paras 3,4, 6.
41 Oddly the MHO has no legal duty to inform the named person of reviews although it would be good practice to do so.
42 The District Courts will be replaced by justice of the peace courts in Scotland from 2008 and be administered by the Scottish Court Service.
43 section 294. Given there is a planning element in a removal order; it would be rare to justify using a justice of the peace.
44 section 35(2)(a).
45 section 293 (3)(a) & (3)(c)(ii).
46 section 293(5).
47 section 295.
48 Scottish Statutory Instruments. 2005/ No.430.
49 see section 254(7) for definition.
50 section 255(5).
51 Tribunal Rule 56(2) under Notices; section 65(4).
52 section 85; 89; 93; section 133 subsection 57C, p. 100.
53 section 255(5).

Index

Introduction

Given this is a book primarily for an MHO, the Index will be divided as follows:

MHO Index

This will follows the legal pathways in the Act in sequence listing the MHO roles of duties after being consulted by the RMO. The main book page reference will be in bold where applicable.

General Index

This will record the main concepts and orders in the Act in alphabetical order. Page references in bold are the key texts.

MHO Index

Notes on section 112 & section 114:

Section 112
This consent applies where a patient in subject to community-based CTO measures and is non-compliant. The patient can initially be brought to any clinic/hospital to receive treatment and an assessment for up to 6 hours. This power only applies if the patient has failed to attend for treatment, for example, section 66(1)(c).

Section 114
This applies when the patient has been non-compliant with any of the other community-based measures. This lasts for up to 28 days and is similar to a short-term detention certificate. The RMO can use this period to assess/treat and if necessary, apply to the Tribunal to vary the measures, for example, to keep the patient in hospital for 6 months.

Section 113
Before implementing this 28-day detention, the RMO has to bring the patient to hospital for 72 hours. This power applies where the patient has been non-compliant with any of the measures, including attendance for treatment. The RMO can then examine the patient and decide whether or not the 28-day detention is appropriate. This is similar to an emergency detention certificate. The main difference is the patient has to remain in hospital for the full 72 hours and then either return home under the community-based CTO or be detained for another 28 days under section 114. MHO consent is not required. So effectively the patient is then detained for 72 hours + 28 days.

These detentions apply to CTOs and interim CTOs., the community-based CTO are also suspended while patient is detained by either section 113 and section 114.

Note: If the patient returns to hospital on a voluntary basis whilst subject to a community-based CTO and then later wishes to leave the hospital, the RMO should consider using the normal short-term detention civil compulsory powers to keep them in hospital. The legal anomaly however is the patient's community-based CTO cannot be suspended if a short-term detention certificate is imposed. The RMO/MHO should therefore seek legal advice. This may become an issue for the Tribunal if the RMO chooses to vary the CTO.

General Index [legal reference to the Act in brackets where applicable]

Footnote:

Suspension certificate. Other civil certificates and one type of criminal prodeeding order an also be suspended. Legal/code of practice page references are as follows:

i) Emergency detention certificate [s.41] volume 1. page 208
ii) Short-term detention certificates[s.53] volume 1, page 50
iii) Compulsory treatment order[s.127] volume 1, page 108
iv) Compulsion orders + interim COs [s.179] volume 3, page 166